Developing Cognitive Bots Using the IBM Watson Engine

Practical, Hands-on Guide to Developing Complex Cognitive Bots Using the IBM Watson Platform

Navin Sabharwal
Sudipta Barua
Neha Anand
Pallavi Aggarwal

Apress®

Developing Cognitive Bots Using the IBM Watson Engine

Navin Sabharwal
New Delhi, India

Sudipta Barua
New Delhi, India

Neha Anand
Varanasi, India

Pallavi Aggarwal
Noida, India

ISBN-13 (pbk): 978-1-4842-5554-4
https://doi.org/10.1007/978-1-4842-5555-1

ISBN-13 (electronic): 978-1-4842-5555-1

Managing Director, Apress Media LLC: Welmoed Spahr
Acquisitions Editor: Celestin Suresh John
Development Editor: James Markham
Coordinating Editor: Aditee Mirashi

Cover designed by eStudioCalamar

Cover image designed by Freepik (www.freepik.com)

Distributed to the book trade worldwide by Springer Science+Business Media New York, 233 Spring Street, 6th Floor, New York, NY 10013. Phone 1-800-SPRINGER, fax (201) 348-4505, e-mail orders-ny@springer-sbm.com, or visit www.springeronline.com. Apress Media, LLC is a California LLC and the sole member (owner) is Springer Science + Business Media Finance Inc (SSBM Finance Inc). SSBM Finance Inc is a **Delaware** corporation.

For information on translations, please e-mail rights@apress.com, or visit http://www.apress.com/rights-permissions.

Apress titles may be purchased in bulk for academic, corporate, or promotional use. eBook versions and licenses are also available for most titles. For more information, reference our Print and eBook Bulk Sales web page at http://www.apress.com/bulk-sales.

Any source code or other supplementary material referenced by the author in this book is available to readers on GitHub via the book's product page, located at www.apress.com/978-1-4842-5554-4. For more detailed information, please visit http://www.apress.com/source-code.

Printed on acid-free paper

Dedicated to the people I love and the God I trust.
—Navin Sabharwal

Dedicated to my family and friends.
—Neha Anand

Dedicated to my mentor and my family.
—Sudipta Barua

Table of Contents

About the Authors

Navin Sabharwal has more than 20 years of industry experience and is an innovator, thought leader, patent holder, and author in the areas of cloud computing, artificial intelligence and machine learning, public cloud, DevOps, AIOPS, infrastructure services, monitoring and management platforms, big data analytics, and software product development. Navin is responsible for DevOps, artificial intelligence, cloud lifecycle management, service management, monitoring and management, IT Ops analytics, AIOPs, and machine learning, automation, operational efficiency of scaled delivery through lean Ops, strategy, and delivery for HCL Technologies. He is reachable at Navinsabharwal@gmail.com and www.linkedin.com/in/navinsabharwal.

Sudipta Barua has worked across various industries in her career, in which the focus has been on driving experiential interface and platforms for end users. She has worked in roles across customer engagements and centricity, marketing, CRM and analytics, PLM and product development. In her current role, Sudipta orchestrates at the intersection of digital marketing, creative storytelling, analytics-driven content development, and experience-driven platforms. She has won numerous awards for her work in leveraging different technology products and solutions to elevate the end-user experience. She is reachable at sudipta.barua.13@gmail.com and https://www.linkedin.com/in/sudipta-barua-022b832/.

Neha Anand is a cognitive solutions architect. She is experienced in managing the delivery lifecycle of enterprise cloud and cognitive solutions. She has implemented and worked on chat bots using various cognitive engines, including Watson, LUIS, LEX, and Dialogflow. She has experience with conversational modeling using natural language processing and machine learning building on bots, and she has worked in development and integration environments. Neha works on developing avenues to drive end-to-end solution and leverage leavers of cognitive, AI, and ML solutions. She is reachable at NehaAnand0511@gmail.com and https://www.linkedin.com/in/neha-anand-05.

Pallavi Aggarwal is a solutions architect for Automation. She has worked on the development and integration of various automation projects using natural language processing and machine learning. She is experienced in the development of various cognitive chatbots. She is reachable at pallaviaggarwal123@gmail.com and www.linkedin.com/in/pallavi-aggarwal-1003

About the Technical Reviewer

Amit Agrawal is a principal data scientist currently working in HCL-DRYiCE. He is based out of Noida and holds master's degree in technology and information security from the Motilal Nehru Institute of Technology (MNNIT)–Allahabad. He has experience in big data systems, such as Apache Hadoop and Apache HBase. He has architected HCL-DRYiCE AI products using NLP and machine learning.

Acknowledgments

To my family, Shweta and Soumil, for being by my side and letting me sacrifice time for my intellectual and spiritual pursuits, and for taking care of everything while I am immersed in authoring. This and other accomplishments of my life wouldn't have been possible without your love and support. To my Mom and my sister for the love and support as always; without your blessings, nothing is possible.

To my coauthors Neha, Pallavi, and Sudipta—thank you for the hard work and quick turnarounds to deliver this. It was an enriching experience; looking forward to working with you again soon.

To my team at HCL, who has been a source of inspiration with their hard work, ever-engaging technical conversations, and technical depth. Your ever-flowing ideas are a source of happiness and excitement every single day. Piyush Pandey, Sarvesh Pandey, Amit Agrawal, Vasand Kumar, Punith Krishnamurthy, Sandeep Sharma, Amit Dwivedi, Gauarv Bhardwaj, Nitin Narotra, Shoyeb, Divjot, Nitin Chand, and Vivek—thank you for being there and making technology fun.

To Celestine and Aditee and the entire team at Apress for turning our ideas into reality. It has been an amazing experience authoring with you; and over the years, the speed of decision-making and the editorial support has been excellent.

To all that I have had the opportunity to work with—my co-authors, colleagues, managers, mentors, and guides, in this world of 7 billion people, it was a coincidence that brought us together. It was and is an enriching experience to be associated with you and learn from you. All ideas and paths are an assimilation of conversations that I have had and experiences I have shared. Thank you.

ACKNOWLEDGMENTS

Thank you goddess Saraswati for guiding me to the path of knowledge and spirituality, and keep me on this path till salvation.

असतो मा साद गमय, तमसो मा ज़्योतरि गमय, मृत्योर मा अमृतम् गमय

(Asato Ma Sad Gamaya, Tamaso Ma Jyotir Gamaya, Mrityor Ma Amritam Gamaya)

Lead us from ignorance to truth, lead us from darkness to light, lead us from death to deathlessness.

CHAPTER 1

Introduction to Cognitive Virtual Bots

What was science fiction yesterday is becoming reality today. This is true for many technologies, and the cognitive virtual assistant is one such technology whose time has come.

A couple of years ago, I read a book where the protagonist created a self-learning chat program that had cognitive abilities to respond, just as any human being would. At that time, it looked like a plot that was only relevant to a sci-fi thriller. What was just a concept until a few years ago, however, is now a reality at scale due to the advent of *cognitive virtual assistants*—more commonly known as *chatbots*.

A chatbot is a computer program that converses in natural language via auditory or textual methods, understands the intent of the user, and sends a response based on business rules and organizational data. It demonstrates itself in the same way that a human would during a two-way conversation.

What started as a concept in a 1950 article by Alan Turing in *Computing Machinery and Intelligence* (`https://en.wikipedia.org/wiki/Computing_Machinery_and_Intelligence`), and the 1966 creation of the first chatbot, known as Eliza, has today evolved into a very complex connected ecosystem powered by artificial intelligence (AI) technologies and machine learning algorithms. Today, a chatbot can help its user with ordering a pizza, booking a vacation, buying an insurance policy, or a very complex task like managing the IT infrastructure of an enterprise, and much more.

© Navin Sabharwal, Sudipta Barua, Neha Anand, Pallavi Aggarwal 2020
N. Sabharwal et al., *Developing Cognitive Bots Using the IBM Watson Engine*,
https://doi.org/10.1007/978-1-4842-5555-1_1

With the advent of customer centricity driven by personalized experiences for customers, it is imperative for enterprises today to be able to sustain relevant conversations with their end users in a short turnaround time, with a higher degree of personalization, and with zero lag in terms of customer history and profiling. According to Gartner, Inc., 25 percent of customer service operations will use virtual customer assistants by 2020 (`https://www.gartner.com/en/newsroom/press-releases/2018-02-19-gartner-says-25-percent-of-customer-service-operations-will-use-virtual-customer-assistants-by-2020`). It further predicts that a virtual chat agent (VCA) is expected to enrich the customer experience, help the customer throughout an interaction, and process transactions on behalf of the customer. Interestingly, the democratization of technology powered by open source platforms from Google, IBM, Facebook, Microsoft, and others allows you to create a chatbot without a professional coder.

If these data points excite you, and you want to explore the possibilities of building your own virtual chat agent, this book is for you.

This book acts as a guide to build your chatbot on the Watson platform developed by IBM. We shall develop chatbots for different use cases for BFSI, travel, the stock market. We will also talk about other cognitive platforms, like LUIS, Lex, and Dialogflow. Further in the book, we explore different bot frameworks, such as Microsoft Bot Framework and Bot Builder.

Let's delve deeper into the topic that is the subject of this book: cognitive virtual assistants. The word *assistant* means someone or something that assists in performing a task or activity. The word *virtual* is a term that is readily identified with software and something that exists in the virtual world. The word *cognitive* relates to the human ability of cognition.

Let's look at how cognition has been defined. Cognition is "the mental action or process of acquiring knowledge and understanding through thought, experience, and the senses." It encompasses many aspects of intellectual functions and processes, such as attention, the formation of knowledge, memory and working memory, judgment and evaluation, reasoning and computation, problem solving and decision making, comprehension, and the production of language. Cognitive processes use existing knowledge and generate new knowledge.

In simple terms, cognition is the human ability that helps us acquire knowledge, perform all our mental functions, understand our environment, and create new knowledge.

Cognitive or intelligent virtual assistants aspire to be more human-like and have similar capabilities that humans have, albeit we still have miles to go before that becomes reality.

Cognitive virtual agents (CVAs) possess some of the capabilities mentioned, but they may not have the ability to compete with humans when it comes to understanding the vast array of contexts there are in our world. However, there are certain areas in which they supersede humans, because they do not have the biological limitations of processing power, and they can scale and communicate with millions of users simultaneously, which a human being cannot.

Let's define a cognitive virtual assistant. A CVA is a software agent that performs tasks for an individual or a system based on text, voice, gestures, or visual input. It has varying degrees of ability to understand the input provided, interpret the input, apply step-by-step logic, probe the user for the intent and context of the conversation, and as a result, provide information or execute the intended task. It can understand a conversation in natural language and maintain the context of the conversation to achieve the objective.

Some CVAs are able to interpret voice commands by first using speech to text, while others can recognize images and take actions accordingly. When it comes to responding, a CVA can respond using text when the mode of communication is a messaging system, it can use voice to respond over voice channels, and it could show gestures, expressions, or movements to express itself in a robotic appearance. CVAs are also embedded in devices like speakers and automobile navigation systems. Some specific voice-enabled examples of these devices are Google Home and Amazon Echo.

CVAs are available on multiple devices and interfaces, and can be accessed via mobile handheld devices, laptops, or PCs. They can also be accessed through different messaging platforms, like Facebook Messenger, Skype, Telegram, and so forth.

CVAs are embedded for mass use as mobile applications, which are called *digital personal assistants*. A few examples of digital personal assistants are Siri by Apple, Google Assistant by Google, and Cortana by Microsoft. Digital personal assistants help users with tasks such as search, navigation, and communication. Digital personal assistants need to be activated with a command so that they know that the user is trying to initiate a conversation. Some examples of these voice commands are "OK Google," "Alexa," and so forth.

Virtual assistants can be leveraged to provide a variety of services. The following are a few examples.

- Act as a search and retrieve agent to retrieve results from various sources for things like weather, stock updates, market information, prices, catalogs, interest rate, and so forth.

- Act as configuration agents to configure alerts, alarms, create to-do lists, shopping lists, travel itineraries, and so forth.

- Play videos or music from catalogs and subscriptions, such as Spotify, Netflix, Amazon Prime, and so forth.

- Act as an IT service desk agent to resolve problems and issues with IT equipment.

- Act as an assistant in specialized services, such as healthcare, legal, administration, and finance.

- Act as an embedded agent in devices (speakers, televisions, and other equipment).

- Act as agents in vehicles and cars to aid with navigation and operate entertainment devices such as music players and so forth.

Privacy Concerns with Cognitive Virtual Assistants

There are obvious and practical security concerns with CVAs. A few consumer cognitive virtual assistants are always in "listen mode," waiting for the voice activation keyword. This means that private conversations between humans are constantly hitting the CVA's microphone. The consumer CVA companies are recording some of the data and using it for training the system to detect human voice and intent better. After all, the deep learning systems working behind the scenes in CVAs need massive amounts of real data to be trained and improved.

Since the CVAs work on audio commands, it is possible to trick them or hack them by embedding audio commands that are undetectable by the human ear, by embedding these commands in music, or spoken text played out from an electronic device. These can be used to manipulate the CVA to do actions controlled by a hacker. Another risk associated with CVAs is that hackers can manipulate virtual assistants to gain entry into systems, as well as physical access into homes and offices.

AI technology provides capabilities like CVAs but also makes it easier to impersonate and re-create someone's voice signature. Today, there are technologies that can create a fake video of someone with an exact voice signature; this technology is getting better by the day.

These concerns have become news headlines in the recent past. The makers of CVAs have come out with recommendations for usage, which provide users better control of whether their data is stored and if it used by the provider or not. As consumers of these systems, we should be well informed about the risk of private data loss. We should be aware of how to use systems in accordance with our privacy needs.

Developer Platforms for CVAs

There are multiple platforms where you can utilize the core technology for creating CVAs and create custom virtual assistants for use by an enterprise. The following lists some of the popular platforms.

- IBM Watson is a suite of artificial intelligence products. It offers conversation, translation, and other APIs along with an out-of-the-box solution called Watson Assistant to quickly create and configure a cognitive virtual assistant.

- Amazon Lex and Polly are tools provided by Amazon Web Services (AWS) to rapidly create and configure a cognitive virtual assistant. AWS has other offerings to help users enhance the capabilities of a CVA.

- Google provides Dialogflow for developers to create compelling virtual agents. It also provides other services, including language translation and speech recognition to enhance the basic features of a cognitive virtual assistant.

Bots vs. Cognitive Virtual Assistants

There are various terms that are used today in the technology space; most popular among them are chatbots, virtual agents, virtual assistants, and bots. Although these terms sound similar, there are major differences in their functionality and features. Let's try to understand these terms.

- *Bot* is a short form of *robot*. It defines any automated program that runs over the Internet. You may have heard of terms like *Twitter bots* and *chatbots*. They are specific examples of bots or software robots that provide a specific type of functionality. Chatbots are specific types of software robots that provide automated responses to user queries or any other type of conversation.

- A virtual assistant is a specific type of a bot that performs the function of an assistant and assists the user with functions that he intends to perform; for example, set an alarm clock, block calendars, read email, play songs, and so forth.

- Both chatbots and virtual assistants can be scripted or have artificial intelligence features. When they are plain scripts, and they do not use natural language understanding (NLU), they are not considered a cognitive chatbot or a cognitive virtual assistant.

The following are features and functions of cognitive chatbots or cognitive virtual agents.

- Natural language understanding capabilities, which means that the bot has the intelligence to understand the intent of the query or conversation.

- Machine learning capabilities that learn from models; the basic input includes multiple chat conversations, dictionaries, and language corpuses.

- The ability to learn from mistakes and increase its understanding of the context and intent of a conversation.

- The ability to integrate with other AI-based services, such as spell checkers, language translation, and tone analyzers. These additional AI services make the cognitive chatbot or assistant very powerful, as compared to an ordinary chatbot or assistant.

- The ability to have more human-like conversations, since all the above features make the cognitive agents more human-like in their conversations as compared to ordinary bots.

- Natural language generation (NLG) capabilities; these bots can generate conversation responses as per the personality of the user who is conversing with a chatbot.

Another significant difference occurs in maintaining the conversational flow. While interacting with a chatbot, if you break the conversation, then the bot will fail to remember the context of the interaction. On the other hand, a virtual assistant utilizes the dynamic conversation flow technique to understand human intent, thus enriching the conversation with humans.

Impact on the Enterprises and Ecosystem

Traditionally, enterprises have used websites and web applications as a means of providing information and gathering information from customers. Think of any enterprise service today, and you would see that it has a website and various applications that are available to authorized users to consume. User experience is the mantra today for any digital enterprise, and they have been investing heavily to make it better by leveraging various technology innovations. In today's world, digital enterprises have two goals in mind. The first is to become more efficient by reducing cycle time and cost, and the other is to enhance the user experience. Cognitive virtual assistants are now becoming a key technology to solve both needs.

Cognitive assistants are delivering an improved user experience along with improved security, simpler business processes, and the reduction of monotonous work for human agents who can thus be trained to solve problems that are more complex. Cognitive virtual agents are becoming the first line of defense, and human agents are becoming the fallback when a CVA is unable to answer a query or solve a problem for the end user.

More and more websites are now having virtual assistants as the front-end interaction interface for customers, where they can seek information, provide input, search for specific content on the website, assist with navigation, fill out forms, request services, and updates. Some of these are powered by cognitive technology while others are simple scripted bots. Cognitive assistants are being adopted rapidly, and most large organizations have implemented or are in the process of implementing cognitive virtual assistant technologies.

Use Cases for Cognitive Virtual Assistants
Self Service/Helpdesk for IT Services

Self-service for IT services by leveraging cognitive virtual assistants is a use case, which has tremendous potential to reduce the effort of IT helpdesk teams. In a hyper competitive environment, it is a priority for most organizations to reduce the cost of delivering IT services while at the same time ensuring that the users get the best of the services.

Since a CVA is available online 24x7 and can handle hundreds of simultaneous conversations, any peaks in an IT service desk where people are waiting for a response are done away with. With the self-service capabilities that a CVA provides, users can solve most of their queries or problems related to laptop, desktop, email, Microsoft Office suite, or other enterprise applications.

Simple but often very voluminous use cases, like password reset or help with accessing an application, can easily be done by CVAs, thus freeing up time of IT resources to help the users with problems that are more complex.

Since IT cuts across verticals, the use cases created here can be leveraged across multiple industry verticals. Many verticals (including banking and financial services, travel, healthcare, hospitality, and retail) are already on the path to deploying CVAs for IT service desk use cases.

A few bots come bundled with IT service desk use cases for readymade consumption with faster time to adoption. One such bot framework is DRYiCE Lucy, which provides hundreds of out-of-the-box use cases for IT (`www.dryice.ai/`).

Triage

There are many use cases under the triage category. Some of the IT service desk use cases also fall under triage. A Triage CVA can ask and probe a user about the issue that he is facing, and can then route or triage him to the right information or to the right human agent to resolve the problem.

To better understand triage use cases, think of it as an intelligent IVR. An IVR asks the user to select an option on telephony networks, and based on the options selected, it provides the information or routes to a human agent. An IVR system with a telecom company, broadband company, or a bank is a good example of how triaging works.

Organizations can take advantage of the CVA capabilities to turn IVR into intelligent communication, and thus elevate the user's experience. Intelligent CVAs can decipher what the user wants and can provide the right information much faster than an IVR. Since CVAs can be integrated with enterprise applications, things like looking up information such as an account balance or a securities balance is easy to implement with a CVA.

Lead Generation

Lead generation, which was thought to be an activity that requires humans to do majority of the tasks, is fast becoming automated.

Lead generation CVAs are mostly embedded within a website. When you land on any page of an organization's website, a popup for a CVA opens and starts a conversation with the visitor.

The use of CVAs as the lead generation front end on websites is quickly catching up, and these days, most websites have a CVA assisting visitors with information.

The benefit of a CVA on websites is that visitors get to know the information quickly and intuitively, and they don't have to go through the entire website and navigate from page to page to get the required information.

In this scenario, since the visitor is interacting with a CVA, the user is no longer a passive visitor but an active visitor who is providing information through chat conversations, which can then be used as a lead, feedback, and so forth.

Ecommerce

Ecommerce virtual assistants are helping millions of consumers to browse, select, and buy products and services with an intuitive interface.

With millions of products listed on ecommerce websites, it is becoming difficult for users to search and find goods and services that they intend to buy. CVAs, which have extensive capabilities to use machine learning technologies to converse and speedily search information, are making buying and selling online easier.

Ecommerce CVAs have extensions and capabilities that include algorithms that match a buyer and a seller.

With CVAs, the complete transaction becomes natural and two-way, in contrast to a website that is static and does not have a conversational flow.

Imagine a scenario where you are asking about a product, and the CVA can pinpoint and show you the exact product that you want. On a static website, if the price was not up to your expectations, you may not buy the product. However, a CVA may look up other offers and provide you a better price—based on an intelligent algorithm. This elevates the user experience multifold.

Integration with Enterprise Applications

Most of us are familiar with the popular virtual assistants programmed into our smartphones or speakers, such as Apple's Siri and Amazon's Echo (Alexa). On the enterprise side, we see leading SaaS companies integrating popular messaging bots like Facebook Messenger into their applications. Major ERP providers such as SAP and Oracle are developing virtual assistants for their applications as well. Some examples of chatbots in this space include the Einstein Bot from Salesforce.

Task Tracking and Project Management

Task management, reminders, and reporting are typical activities in a project.

Cognitive virtual assistants can look up information, collate information, and integrate with enterprise project management systems, which make them ideal for simplifying and automating the project management process.

Users can use a CVA for setting alerts, requesting project status, scheduling meetings, and searching project-related documents. CVAs with machine learning capabilities can easily accomplish all of these tasks.

Today, projects span across multiple geographies and time zones, and coordination with multiple teams can become a challenge for project managers. With the automation provided from using CVAs, what was once complex is now simple.

CVAs integrate with most enterprise project management tools to automate processes and to provide an intuitive, easy-to-use user interface for project managers, coordinators, and team members.

CVAs may not yet be intelligent enough to plan a project or to make decisions, but in the near future, such complex tasks may well be within the reach of an AI-driven CVA.

Human Resources

Most processes in human resources—from hiring through the employee lifecycle—are pretty standardized these days. Most enterprises have automated these processes using ERP products.

CVAs are a natural fit in HR processes. Recruitment, day-to-day employee interactions, query solving, appraisal cycles, and more can be fully automated with cognitive virtual assistants.

CVAs handle shortlisting candidates, scheduling interviews, ensuring that interviews happen, getting feedback from interviews, assisting with filling out required information forms, and more.

CVAs are also used in the onboarding process once an employee joins an organization. This is a task that requires the CVA to take the employee through the various policies and procedures.

Most new employees have questions and they rely on their colleagues or buddies to get this information. With a CVA deployed, the task becomes faster and eliminates dependencies. This results in faster onboarding and a better employee experience. On an ongoing basis, queries related to processes, policies, changes in policies, leaves, travel, emoluments, benefits, insurance, and HR-related areas can be answered by CVAs with accuracy and a shorter turnaround time.

Conclusion

Now that we have discussed cognitive virtual assistants and their uses, we are ready to build our own virtual assistant by leveraging the Watson platform. But before we do that, let's deep dive into Watson.

CHAPTER 2

Various Cognitive Platforms/Engines

Artificial intelligence (AI) has taken the digital world by storm. AI is increasingly relevant in a varied set of applications and use cases. It is used in a variety of personal digital assistants, including Siri, Cortana, Alexa, and Google Assistant, for solving consumers' day-to-day use cases. *Cognitive computing* defines a system that tries to simulate the way a human mind works. These two terms use the same technologies, including machine learning, neural networks, natural language processing, and sentimental analysis. IBM defines cognitive computing as "systems that learn at scale, reason with purpose, and interact with humans naturally." Cognitive computing focuses on human machine interaction by using self-learning algorithms to enable decision-making and to make life easier for humans.

Colloquially, the term *artificial intelligence* is applied when a machine mimics cognitive functions that humans associate with *the* human mind, such as learning, reasoning, and problem solving.

Watson

Watson is IBM's suite of enterprise-ready AI services, applications, and tooling. It is a collection of cloud services running on the IBM Cloud platform aimed at delivering exceptional performance. Watson uses natural language processing, natural language understanding, and

© Navin Sabharwal, Sudipta Barua, Neha Anand, Pallavi Aggarwal 2020
N. Sabharwal et al., *Developing Cognitive Bots Using the IBM Watson Engine*,
https://doi.org/10.1007/978-1-4842-5555-1_2

machine learning to convert large amounts of unstructured data into something tangible and insightful.

Watson gained recognition when it defeated world champions Ken Jennings and Brad Rutter on the *Jeopardy* television gameshow. Since *Jeopardy* covers a vast spectrum of subjects, it showcased Watson's ability to go beyond analyzing databases (versus a more complex system of algorithms), continuous learning models, hypotheses, and decision-making powers that qualified Watson to win the game. Watson is said to be a supercomputer that can mirror human cognition process by dividing it into four different sections.

The first section is the ability to *observe*. Watson learns information from a variety of web sources and a vast repository of databases in a millionth of a second.

The second section is the ability to *interpret*. Watson consumes all the information it has received and processes it into a format that is more efficient and easier to process. Since a computer only understands binary, Watson calibrates the data—whether text, speech, or images—into binary. However, at this step, Watson relies on a human to instruct it as to how to interpret this information. This is done by a Q&A model in which Watson is trained to understand the meaning of the data beyond the facts it has been exposed to, and then logically constructs the relationships between the facts.

The third section is *evaluation*, where Watson can evaluate the relevance of the information based on the feedback it receives from the sources that it gathered the information from. It can filter out the irrelevant information based on a scoring system.

The fourth section is *decision*. After evaluating the accuracy of the information, Watson can build on a variety of patterns regarding the existing patterns of the information in a way that is similar to what a human brain would do. This enables Watson to gather information, process it intelligently, and solve problems related to the subject it is working on. Through its hypothesis and evidence scoring, Watson can not only suggest possible solutions based on its established information from external sources, but based on what it has learned, it can align a confidence score and thus intelligently decide on the best solution for the problem it is working on.

Products and Services

With the help of the Watson Assistant service, we can build applications and agents that can understand natural language input and simulate a conversation with the end user that emulates a human-to-human conversation. The elements for building an AI-enabled ecosystem is depicted in Figure 2-1.

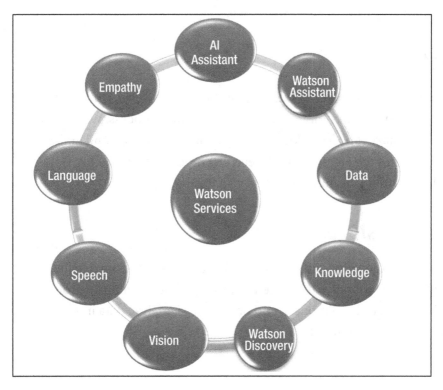

Figure 2-1. *Watson services*

AI Assistant

An assistant enables you to route the end user's request to the best possible solution. This capability integrates the channels dedicated to help solve the end user's request, and makes it easier to manage requests.

Watson Assistant

Watson Assistant is an offering for building conversational interfaces into any application, device, or channel. It knows when to search for an answer from a knowledge warehouse, when to ask for clarification, and when to direct the user to a human assistant. Watson Assistant runs on the IBM cloud, thus allowing businesses to bring AI, scalability, and agility together to enhance the end user's experience.

Data

An organization's smartest resource is its data. However, generating value out of the data is a complex and time-consuming process. Watson Data services make it possible for the user to collect, organize, and analyze data. It automates the creation of self-learning models, data labeling, data bias reduction, data cleaning, and data visualization.

Watson Studio

Watson Studio helps you to extract value and insights from data by enabling collaborative data science and machine learning environments to build and train AI models, and prepare and analyze data in a single integrated environment.

Watson Machine Learning

This service empowers you to use the data to create, train, and deploy self-learning models. It leverages an automated, collaborative workflow to build intelligent applications.

Watson Knowledge Catalog

The Watson Knowledge Catalog is a collaborative asset catalog that is designed to discover and categorize enormous volumes of data spread across disparate sources.

Watson OpenScale

Watson OpenScale is a scalable platform that gives the user a clear and accurate view of their AI systems, which helps to track and refine their performance across its lifecycle.

Knowledge

In the space of artificial intelligence, learning, and knowledge gathering is a continuous process. The AI system does not rely on deriving outcomes on the data repository or pre-existing run books, but works on building a newer knowledge repository through collaborative learning over each interaction, just like the human brain. Watson Knowledge services enable in developing this holistic evolving knowledge system.

Watson Discovery

Watson Discovery is an AI search technology that eliminates data silos and retrieves information buried inside enterprise data. Watson Discovery applies the latest breakthroughs in machine learning, including natural language processing and natural language understanding capabilities, and it is easily trained to the users' domain. With the flexibility of the IBM Cloud, users can operate anywhere providing it scale and agility. The user can even train it for a particular domain by using Watson Knowledge Studio.

Watson Discovery News

The outcome of data churning is not only a function of the data itself but is also influenced by other environmental factors. For example, if there were news of a country being hit by a virus that is only curable by a particular drug, the stock price of that drug would invariably rise. Watson Discovery news is a powerful tool with the ability to build such intelligence into an AI system. It is an indexed dataset that is pre-enriched with the following cognitive insights: keyword extraction, entity extraction, semantic role extraction, sentiment analysis, relation extraction, and category classification. To make the system more robust, the historical search is available for the past 60 days of news data.

Watson Natural Language Understanding (NLU)

The volume of unstructured data is multiplying manifold every moment thanks to the advent of social media and other such channels. It has become difficult to understand the complexities of the human language due to this data explosion. Watson Natural Language Understanding is a set of refined natural language capabilities with advanced text analytics to derive insights like relationships, keywords, and sentiments from such unstructured data and create meaningful outcomes.

Watson Knowledge Studio

This service enables to teach Watson to discover meaningful insights in unstructured data without writing any code. This allows the domain SMEs in any field to work collaboratively to empower Watson to understand the language specific to that domain or industry. For example, the definition of a virus in medical science is very different from the meaning of a virus in the cybersecurity ecosystem. It also enables Watson to apply the knowledge it has acquired across multiple applications by using models from Watson Knowledge Studio in Watson Discovery, Watson Natural Language Understanding, and Watson Explorer.

Vision

As humans, a lot of what we learn is through the things that we see. However, for a computer system it is very hard to understand such visual data, let alone classify and analyze such complex data set.

Watson is built with the Watson Visual Recognition service, which understands visual data and organizes large volumes of visual data into structured, labeled data sets. Watson is trained using a set of related data. For example, you may want to teach Watson to recognize a car from a truck. Watson Visual Recognition needs to be exposed to a variety of car and truck images so that it can tell you if the random image that you expose Watson to is a car or a truck. This complex feature is very significant and takes Watson's capabilities to the next level of intelligence.

Speech

Like visuals, speech is another significant platform for data generation. Humans seamlessly interact with each other using speech as a medium to generate, document and understand data. Watson's Speech to Text and Text to Speech services not only help in converting data from one format to another, it also enables Watson to understand different dialects, pronunciations, languages and talk back to the user in a human-like voice. The Speech to Text service automates converting spoken data to written transcripts. Similarly, textual data generated by the Watson engine can be delivered in form of a real human-like conversational to the end user, thus enhancing the user experience and the user journey.

LUIS

LUIS (Language Understanding Intelligence Service) is a Microsoft service that provides a cloud-based API services that bring custom Machine Learning Intelligence to a user's conversation and in decoding Natural Language text to predict the meaning of the conversation. Basically, a client application for LUIS is a conversational application that communicates with a user in natural language to complete a task.

LUIS uses machine learning models to allow developers to build applications that can receive user input in a natural language and extract meaning from it. Prototyped to identify valuable information in conversations, LUIS interprets user goals and extracts valuable information from entities resulting in high quality as a language model. LUIS synchronizes easily with the Azure Bot Service, making it easy to create a sophisticated bot.

A LUIS application contains a domain-specific natural language model. There are various ways to compile a LUIS app, including prebuilt domain models, custom models, or blending a prebuilt domain with custom information. LUIS has many prebuilt domain models, including intents, utterances, and entities. It also helps with creating the entire design. LUIS has several ways to identify custom intents and entities, including machine learning entities, specific or literal entities, or a combination of machine learning entities and literals.

Azure Products and Services

With the help of Azure Bot service, we can build applications and agents that can decipher natural language input and simulate a conversation with end users that emulates a human to human conversation. The elements of building such an AI-enabled ecosystem of cognitive services are depicted in Figure 2-2.

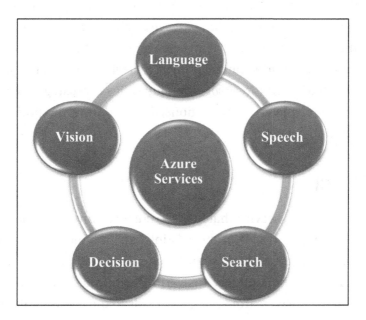

Figure 2-2. *Azure Services*

Language

Language is the basic element that ensures that applications and services can fully understand the value of unstructured text or can recognize the intent behind a speaker's utterances. It is divided into three parts: Text Analytics, QnA Maker, and Translator Text API.

Text Analytics

Text Analytics is a cloud-based service that provides advanced natural language processing over input text, along with processing four major functions: sentiment analysis, key phrase extraction, language detection, and entity recognition.

Sentiment analysis[1] discovers a customer's gestures by analyzing raw text, whether it is positive or negative. *Key phrase extraction* identifies the main points in the phrase. *Language detection* deciphers the variant in which the text is written, and converts a single language code for every document submitted on the request in a wide range of languages, variants, and dialects. *Entity recognition* identifies and categorizes entities as people,[2] places, organizations, date and time, quantities, percentages, and currencies.

QnA Maker

This is a cloud-based service that helps to create a conversational question/answer platform over the existing data. It builds a knowledge base by extracting queries from semistructured content, which includes FAQs, manuals, and documents. Answering users' questions with the best possible answers from the QnAs leads to the creation of the knowledge base. The best part of QnA Maker is that it becomes smarter as it constantly learns from user behavior.

---

[1]https://docs.microsoft.com/en-in/azure/cognitive-services/
text-analytics/how-tos/text-analytics-how-to-sentiment-analysis
[2]https://docs.microsoft.com/en-in/azure/cognitive-services/
text-analytics/how-tos/text-analytics-how-to-entity-linking

Translator Text

Translator Text is a machine translation service that is easy to integrate into applications, websites, tools, and solutions. It allows developers to add multilanguage user experiences in more than 60 languages,[3] and it can be used for text-to-text language translation.

Speech Service

Speech is another significant platform of data generation. Humans seamlessly interact with each other using speech as a medium to generate, document and understand data. Speech services are the union of audio-to-text, speech translation, and text-to-speech capabilities. We can also say that it converts spoken language into text, or it produces natural information speech from text using standard voice. It also provides a speaker recognition service that identifies individual speakers or uses speech as an authentication mechanism, since every individual voice has unique characteristics that can identify a person, just like a figure print.

Search

The search service in LUIS gives the applications the power and the ability to search across huge quantum of ad free information across the web. It helps to find the exact requirements from billions of webpages, images, videos, and news search results.

Bing Spell Check

Bing Spell Check performs contextual grammar and spell checks. Bing has developed a web-based spell-checker that has machine learning and

---

[3]https://docs.microsoft.com/en-in/azure/cognitive-services/translator/languages

statistical machine translation capabilities. It is based on a massive body of web searches and documents, and it can help users check spelling errors and slang and recognize the differences between names and brand names, and so forth.

Bing Web Search

It is a RESTful service that provides instant resolution to user queries. Search results are easily configured to include web pages, images, videos, news and more. Bing Web Search provides the results based on search relevance with subscriptions.

Bing Entity Search

Bing Entity Search sends a search query to Bing and gets relevant results, including entities and places. Places include restaurants and other local business hubs. Bing returns places if the query specifies the name of the local business or asks for a type of business (for example, restaurants near me). Bing returns entities if the query specifies well-known people and places (tourist attractions, states, countries, regions).

Decision

The Decision API comes with built-in services, like Content Moderator, Anomaly Detector, and Personalizer. Content Moderator is an Azure Cognitive Service, and it is a machine-assisted content moderation API that augments image, text, and video moderation capabilities. It can detect offensive and unwanted images, racial and adult video content, and profane and undesirable text. When such material is found, the service adds an appropriate label and flags it to the content moderator. The application can then manage the flagged content as per the defined regulations and maintain the planned environment for users. A few examples of where software engineers can use the Content Moderator service are online marketplaces that moderate product catalogs and other user-generated content, gaming companies that moderate user-generated game artifacts and chat rooms, and social messaging platforms that moderate user-generated content in the form of images, text, and videos.

Vision

As humans, a lot of what we learn is through the things that we see. However, for a computer system it is very hard to understand such visual data, let alone classify and analyze such complex data sets. Azure's Cognitive Services make it possible to accurately identify and analyze content within images, videos, and digital ink.

The **Computer Vision** service uses advanced algorithms that process images and return information. To analyze an image, you can either upload an image or specify an image through a URL. Depending on the visual features that users are interested in, image-processing algorithms can analyze the content accordingly and provide insights about their characteristics. From a set of thousands of recognizable objects, living things, scenery, and actions, it identifies visual features in images and can identify commercial brands in images or videos from a database of thousands of global logos.

The **Cognitive Services Face API** provides advanced algorithms that are used to detect, recognize, and analyze human faces in images. Human face information is useful in many different software scenarios. Trending scenarios are security, natural user interfaces, image content analysis and management, mobile apps, and robotics.

Ink Recognizer is an AI service that recognizes digital handwriting, common shapes, and the layout of inked documents. It identifies common geometric shapes—like a polygon in digital ink—along with their geometric hot points and layout coordinates. Ink Recognizer has the potential to add value to notetaking, completing forms, content searches, and document annotation.

Amazon AI Services

Amazon Web Services (AWS) has been a disrupter on how technology can impact and enhance the user experience. With AWS Artificial Intelligence Services, Amazon has manifested that experience. Whether it is a seamless check-in and checkout at a physical Amazon Go store, or getting Alexa to make your coffee, switch on your television, and play music at an end of a tiring day, AWS AI services are getting matured every day with every interaction it is having with its users. AI services from Amazon empowers its users with competencies like natural language, video analysis, virtual assistants, personalized recommendations, and forecasting without requiring to have a deep expertise in machine learning. This is beneficial for businesses since it enables a business to technology conversation and integration easily and enables faster and more value driven outcomes.

Products and Services

The evolution of AI at Amazon started in the late 1990s, when it had a discovery agent that recommended books that a subscriber might like based on her favorite author, genre, or other parameters. Since then, AI at Amazon has evolved and matured, and can now run complex algorithms across natural language understanding, object and facial recognition, chatbots, speech-enabled conversations, automatic speech recognition, and much more. Amazon AI services also address a very important need for the business to scale up artificial intelligence for driving business outcomes. Its AI services can be used in silos or in conjunction with each other, giving the users the speed, agility, and flexibility to run effective business operations and enhance the end user experience.

Amazon Lex

Amazon Lex is a service under Amazon AI where you can build chatbots that can recognize, understand, and chat in speech-to-text or text-to-speech form and can have human-like conversations. Amazon Lex can be used to create conversational interfaces using voice or text as a chat medium. It uses natural language understanding to understand the context of the conversation and automatic speech recognition that can convert speech to text. This enables the user to build advanced chatbot without having the proficiency of complex technologies. Lex uses the same deep learning algorithms that power Amazon Alexa and makes it accessible to developers, thus enabling faster cycle time and ease of development to build sophisticated, natural language-enabled conversational bots. It won't be wrong to say that Lex has democratized deep learning technologies and built smart and responsive bots. Since Lex can easily scale up or down depending on the usage, it brings elasticity to the IT infrastructure required to run the service. The following are additional benefits of Amazon Lex.

- **Ease of use:** It offers an easy-to-use console to quickly build your chatbot. It has predefined bots if you are not familiar with the Amazon Lex console. Lex also has the capability where it can build a complete natural language model even if it is supplied with just a few phrases, Lex can intelligently train the bot to the next level.

- **Seamlessly deployment and scaling:** Using the console, the developer can build, test, and deploy the bot straightaway. It also provides ease of integration to various applications and easily publish the voice or text chatbots to mobile devices, web apps, and chat services such as Facebook Messenger, Slack, Twilio and more. Since Lex is on a SaaS model, the infrastructure is completely elastic, and you don't have to worry about scaling the infrastructure as the user volume and conversations increases or decreases.

- **Cost efficacy:** Lex works on a cost-effective model. Unlike other services, Lex doesn't charge any upfront charges or any minimum fee. It also provides the Amazon Lex free tier so that the user can try Lex without any initial investment. Amazon Lex works on a pay per use model and has a low cost per request, thus optimizing on the cost implications for the user.

- **Built-in integration with AWS:** Lex has many built-in integrations—like Lambda, MobileHub, and CloudWatch—that allow the user to integrate with many other AWS services, like Cognito, DynamoDB, Amazon Poly, and many others. This feature enables Lex to leverage AWS' platforms for monitoring, security, business logic, user authentication, storage, and mobile development.

Amazon Polly

Human speech is one of the most powerful ways to communicate. The same word can have different connotation based on the tonality, context, and pitch of the word that is spoken. AWS Polly is a cloud-based service that uses advanced deep learning technologies to convert text to human-like speech. It can support multiple languages and has a strong repository of life like voices that gives it the agility to be used to build speech-enabled applications and use the appropriate voice depending on the business case and the end user's sentiment. Polly uses a variety of Neural Text to Speech (NTTS) voices, which is evolving and learning every day. The NTTS technology also gives Polly the ability to synthesize a newscaster's speaking style that is personalized to the news narration speaking style. Polly can be used to augment human voice across mobile application, e-learning software, games, accessibility applications for visually impaired, IoT and many other domains. The following are some of the benefits of Polly.

- **Large portfolio of voices and language:** Unlike other services, Polly provides a vast array of languages to choose from. It also has a repository of human-like male and female voices. It offers both NTTS and TTS technology to synthesize the superior natural speech with high pronunciation accuracy.

- **Low latency:** To deliver life-like conversations and conversational experiences, it is imperative that the service has a low latency and fast response time. When text is sent to Polly's API, it returns the audio to the application as a stream so that the voice can be played immediately, thus making the conversation and interaction human-like with low latency.

Amazon Rekognition

AWS's facial recognition technology is called Rekognition. This web-based service makes it possible for developers to add image and video analysis to the applications. With Rekognition services the applications can detect, remember, and understand emotions of the faces and objects in the frame(s). What is even more impressive is that using deep learning technology developed by computer vision scientists, Rekognition can read, analyze, and store the millions of images that it is exposed to every day. It requires no prior knowledge of machine learning.

It can also extract any text that is written in any image or video, such as captions, product names, street names, and so forth. Rekognition is learning the quantum of videos, images, and other visual data that is stored in its repository. It learns from this data while *continuously* labeling the data based on a confidence scoring algorithm.

This service also has the ability to detect activity and scenes beyond recognizing objects. For example, Rekognition has the capability to do real-time and batch video analytics. When Rekognition captures a video, it is not only capturing the particular frame, but it is cognitive enough to capture and understand the frames captured before and after the frame in question, thus contextualizing the content. Rekognition also has the capability to identify inappropriate visual content that the user might not want in the application and provides with detailed labels that help the user to control unwanted content on need basis. It is not only capable of identifying and labeling faces and visual content based on its repository of data that it has acquired, but is also matured enough to know any emotions attached to the facial recognition abilities. This service also has the ability for celebrity recognition.

Another unique Rekognition feature is called *person tracking*. Using a technology called *skeleton modelling*, it tracks whether a person is in the frame or not, even if blocked from the line of vision.

It is important to understand the benefits of the Rekognition service.

- **Low cost:** Like other AWS AI services, Rekognition is built on a pay-as-you-go model, and there is no upfront cost. The user only pays for the images and videos that are analyzed and the face metadata that is stored.

- **Integration with other AWS services:** Rekognition can work seamlessly with other AWS services like Lambda and AWS S3. In response to the AWS S3 event, the Rekognition API can be called directly from Lambda. Because both AWS Lambda and AWS S3 scale automatically basis the response to the application's demand, you can build scalable, affordable, and reliable image analysis applications.

It is also possible to run analytics directly on images that are stored in Amazon S3 without having to load or move the data.

- **Fully managed:** Despite the huge increase in the number of requests, there is a consistency in the latency of the application. This feature ensures a seamless and enriched end-user experience.

Amazon Translate

Amazon Translate is a translation service that removes the complexity of building translation capabilities into the application by calling the Translate API. This enables the developer to build multilingual applications with a single API and a few lines of code. Research shows that the chances of stickiness is higher when individuals are exposed to a conversation or information interface like a website, customer agent, or blogs and post that is in their own native language. To do so manually would mean a long turnaround time, not to mention the high costs involved in the translation of all the digital assets that any organization would have.

Amazon Translate is built on the technology of neural machine translation and automates language translations using deep learning models to translate digital assets with high accuracy and natural-sounding translation based on aspects like local dialects, brand-specific style, language-specific composition, and so on. It uses machine learning and continuous learning to drive accuracy and efficiency over time. Amazon Translate can integrate with other services, like Amazon Comprehend, for extracting predetermined entities, sentiments, or key words from social media or other short-form text. It can also integrate with Amazon Polly to convert to speech and deliver the translated data to the user.

At present Amazon Translate supports 25 languages and supports over almost 600 translation combinations. In cases where the source language of the content is not specified, Translate can detect the source language with high accuracy. It also has the capability to perform batch translation where the volume of data is very large or real-time translation to deliver on demand translation of content like in case of a bot interface.

Amazon Transcribe

Amazon Transcribe leverages the deep learning process called automatic speech recognition service that enables developers to transcribe speech to text. By using this API service, it is possible to analyze an audio file that is stored in Amazon S3 and return the content of the audio file in a transcribed text format.

Historically, we have had to use humans to convert such audio to text transcriptions. With Amazon Transcribe the entire process is automated, scalable, cost effective and has a faster turnaround time. It has the intelligence and the ability to automatically add punctuations and formatting thus making the output more accurate in terms of the conversion. The audio can be processed in batches or in near real time, which means that it is possible to input live stream of audio data and get the output in transcibed text in parallel.

This API puts a timestamp against each word and is quite useful in case you want to find a particular word in the original audio or insert subtitles into a particular slot in a video. Amazon Transcribe is flexible enough for new words to be added to the base vocabulary to generate more accurate transcriptions. This allows addition of domain-specific words and phrases like product names, technical terminology, or names of individuals, places, and so forth. Moreover, Translate can integrate with other Amazon API like Amazon Translate thus enabling localization of audio and audio-enabled video content.

Dialogflow

Dialogflow is a Google-owned platform of human-computer interaction technologies based on natural language conversations. Google provides Speaktoit, a virtual buddy for Android and iOS that performs tasks and answers users' queries in a natural language. Speaktoit has created a natural language processing engine that helps in conversation context like dialogue history, location, and user preferences. It acts as a natural language understanding platform that makes it easy to design and summarize a conversational user interface into any of the platforms like mobile, web, and devices. It also helps in providing new and engaging ways for the users to interact with the products.

This technology is proficient in analyzing multiple inputs at the same time from customers, including text or audio inputs (like from a mobile phone or voice recording). It also helps to revert to the users in a couple of ways, either through text or with synthetic speech. This provides users new ways to interact with the product by building engaging voice and text-based conversational interfaces such as voice apps and chatbots powered by Googles AI technology. This is an end-to-end tool that is powered by natural language understanding to facilitate rich and natural conversations.

Google Products and Services

With the help of the Google AI cognitive service, we can build applications and agents that can decipher natural language input, simulate a conversation with end users, and emulate a human-to-human conversation. The Google services available for us to build cognitive virtual agents are described next.

Speech-to-Text

Google Cloud Speech-to-Text provides developers to convert audio to text by using powerful neural network models in an easy-to-use API. The Speech-to-Text API recognizes 120 languages and versions to support your global user base. This service also has the functionality to enable voice command-and-control, transcribe audio from call centers, and more.

Using Google machine learning technology, it can process real-time streaming or prerecorded audio.

To perform speech recognition, Cloud Speech-to-Text has three main methods.

- **Synchronous recognition:** It sends audio data to the Speech-to-Text API, then performs recognition on that data, and returns results after all audio has been processed. Synchronous recognition requests are limited to audio data of 1 minute or less in duration.

- **Asynchronous recognition:** It sends audio data to the Speech-to-Text API and starts with a Long Running Operation. Using this operation, you can periodically process for recognition results. Asynchronous requests can handle audio data of any duration up to 480 minutes.

- **Streaming recognition:** It performs recognition on audio data provided within a gRPC bidirectional stream.[4] For real-time recognition scenarios, streaming requests are designed and used for recording live audio from a microphone. Streaming recognition provides interval results while audio is being captured, hence allowing the result to appear in between while the user is speaking.

---

[4]http://www.grpc.io/docs/guides/concepts.html#bidirectional-streaming-rpc

Text-to-Speech

Google Cloud Text-to-Speech converts text into speech in more than 180 voices in more than 30 human languages and variants. It applies innovative research in speech synthesis and uses Google's powerful neural network technology to deliver high-fidelity audio. This API makes user interaction easy and can transform customer services, device interaction and many more applications.

Text-to-speech makes it possible for developers to create natural-sounding, synthetic human speech as playable audio. It easily converts arbitrary strings, words, and sentences into the sound of a person speaking. Imagine that you have an application that is a voice assistant with the capability to take feedback from a user as playable audio in natural language. Integrating it with this API, the application might take an action and then provide human speech as feedback to the user.

Language Translation

Language Translation API uses Google's pretrained neural machine translation to deliver fast, powerful results. Within Translation API and same client library, users can now even choose to use custom model translations. Translations is easy to integrate in applications, websites, tools, and solutions. It supports multilanguage user experiences in more than 100 languages,[5] from Afrikaans to Zulu translation, and allows users to build custom models in more than 50 language pairs.

Natural Language

Natural Language Services derives insights from unstructured text using Google machine learning. It uses machine learning to extract the structure

---

[5]https://cloud.google.com/translate/

37

and meaning of a text. With this service, users can extract information about people, places, and events, and can have a better understanding of the social media sentiments and customer conversations. Natural language offers the ability to analyze text and integrate it with your document storage on Google Cloud Storage.

Using AutoML Natural Language, the user can upload their own data and train it on custom, high-quality, machine learning models to classify, extract, and detect sentiment with zero effort by calling an API to get insights that are relevant. The powerful pretrained models of the Natural Language API make development easy by providing functionalities like sentiment analysis, entity analysis, entity sentiment analysis, content classification, and syntax analysis.

Conclusion

This chapter was an introduction to some of the main players in the cognitive virtual assistant space. There are cloud-based services available from IBM Watson, Microsoft Azure, Amazon Web Services, and Google Cloud platform, which we can leverage to create cognitive virtual assistants. Users can evaluate and leverage all required services from a single cloud or opt to leverage a multicloud architecture by choosing the best services across clouds. This space is rapidly changing, knowing which provider provides what services is important for architects and developers to choose the best and most cost-effective options for their needs.

CHAPTER 3

Bot Frameworks

Bot frameworks provide a platform for developers to build intelligent conversational agents (bots) and connect them via messaging channels such as Skype, Facebook Messenger, Slack, Telegram, and so forth.

Bot frameworks combine with cognitive services like Watson, LUIS, Lex, and Dialogflow to provide rich and useful interactions with users.

A bot framework and its integration with cognitive services and channels is depicted in Figure 3-1.

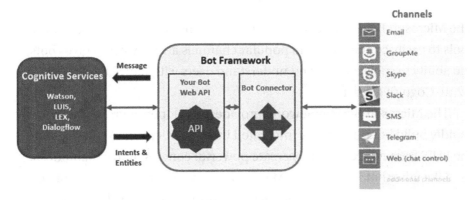

Figure 3-1. *Bot framework architecture*

Bot frameworks help develop and bind the various components of an application. It is a platform interface for building, connecting, testing, and deploying intelligent bots. It helps build and connect intelligent bots to interact with users.

© Navin Sabharwal, Sudipta Barua, Neha Anand, Pallavi Aggarwal 2020
N. Sabharwal et al., *Developing Cognitive Bots Using the IBM Watson Engine*,
https://doi.org/10.1007/978-1-4842-5555-1_3

Connectivity to many channels is one of the features of a bot framework. It supports Skype, Slack, Facebook Messenger, and other such messaging services.

The Bot Connector provides the following services to ease communication between a bot and the user.

- Bot registration

- Connectivity and message routing with a list of channels to reach users

- Conversation and state management

Next, we discuss a few popular bot frameworks and some of their important features. Users can choose a bot framework based on features, pricing, and how it best fits an application's needs.

Microsoft Bot Framework

The Microsoft Bot Framework has a comprehensive open source SDK and tools to easily connect a bot to popular channels and devices. It gives bots the ability to speak, listen, and understand users with native integration to Azure Cognitive Services.

The Microsoft Bot Framework[1] provides developers with SDK to rapidly build bots. It is neatly integrated with the Microsoft AI services and the LUIS framework to rapidly create powerful conversation capabilities.

Like other bot frameworks, Microsoft provides connectors to connect to various messaging platforms, such as Twitter, Slack, and Skype. It has a unique feature where it enables you to search and discover existing bots and the services provided by them.

---

[1]https://dev.botframework.com

The open source Microsoft SDK provides native integration with the Azure Cognitive Services, which makes it simpler and faster for developers to create intuitive conversational bots. The samples and code provided by Microsoft help kick-start bot projects and cuts down on the time required to complete them.

The range of utilities by the Microsoft Bot Framework include translation services integration, conversation state management, debugging tools, and embeddable web chat control. Code samples for various use cases and examples from different domains are available for developers to use.

Microsoft Bot Framework Features

The Microsoft Bot Framework integrates voice, speech, language understanding, translation, and other services available from Azure Cognitive Services. The cloud services from Azure form the backbone of any bot. There is a large community of .NET developers who find it easy to take their framework and language skills in C# to the next level by using the SDK to create cognitive bots.

The SDK is open source and includes lifecycle guidance on how to build, test, and take a bot to production. This lifecycle guidance is unique to the Microsoft Bot Framework and makes it easier for new cognitive bot developers to learn and implement.

Microsoft's repository of enterprise solutions integrate with the Bot Framework, which takes out a lot of plumbing work that may be required in other bot frameworks. This out-of-the-box integration with the Microsoft enterprise ecosystem makes it a good option for Microsoft customers.

Many enterprises are starting to use Cortana, Teams, and Skype as standard collaboration platforms. The deep integration and samples provided with the Microsoft Bot Framework make it easier for developers to leverage the existing deployment of collaboration tools and embed the bot within these tools. Users can continue to use their channel of choice and communicate with the bot with the familiar user interface of an enterprise collaboration platform.

Microsoft Bot Connector

The Bot Connector[2] connects to text/SMS, Office 365 mail, Skype, Slack, and other services (see Figure 3-2).

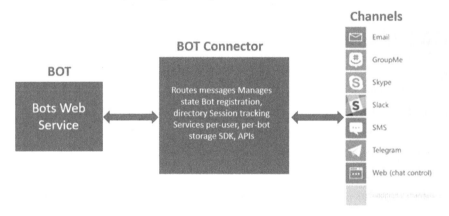

Figure 3-2. Bot Connector

BOT SDK

The open source Microsoft Bot SDK has all the required tools to build a bot, including lifecycle guidance and a large set of samples provided as code and building blocks.

---

[2]https://www.nuget.org/packages/Microsoft.Bot.Connector/

Botpress

Botpress[3] is an open source platform popular among developers. It is a lightweight framework for rapidly prototyping and building conversational bots. Similar to the Microsoft Bot Framework, it comes bundled with various features to make it easier for developers to build bots that can converse over voice and chat channels.

Powered by an expanding community, Botpress boasts a GUI-driven approach to create compelling bots where there is less need to code.

If you are constrained on time and need a lightweight engine to create your bot or are experimenting with bot frameworks, Botpress may be your platform of choice.

Since Botpress is a completely standalone framework (unlike other frameworks), it is flexible, extensible, and integratable with most cognitive offerings.

It is available in-premise, so you don't have to depend on cloud providers. If your use case needs in-premise deployment due to security or compliance concerns, Botpress may be your platform of choice.

Botpress comes with the following components.

- **Natural language understanding (NLU) engine**. It does post processing of text using Natural Language processing Algorithm. Natural language understanding analyzes text to extract the information (concepts, entities, keywords, topics, categories, relationships, and so forth). The structured data is ready to be consumed by the other components. This module comes bundled with the Botpress Framework.

- **Visual flow editor**. Similar to the IBM Watson Assistant, Botpress has its own visual interface

---

[3]https://www.botpress.io

to rapidly prototype and create workflows for conversations. Its simple and intuitive workflow designer can be used by developers to model a conversation flow and test use cases. This means less code and rapid development.

- **Messaging channels**. Botpress supports multiple channels of communication, including Facebook messenger, SMS, and email, which makes it easier for developers to integrate with popular messaging apps.

- **Chat emulator**. The emulator helps developers test their bots and see how the bot responds to various input. It is an essential tool to make bots production grade.

Lucy Bot

Lucy[4] is a cognitive virtual assistant. It mimics human interaction and learns. It adapts to a user's needs through smart conversations by leveraging enterprise-grade natural language processing (NLP) and machine learning (ML).

Lucy finds relevant information available across different enterprise systems. Lucy helps organizations move up the maturity curve and enhance the user experience for employees and customers. By leveraging advanced natural language processing, Lucy reduces human errors and increases productivity. It comes with out-of-the-box use cases for various scenarios, and it can be easily extended to cover the "cognitive chatbot" needs of modern enterprises.

The three key components of Lucy's architecture are shown in Figure 3-3.

---

[4]https://www.dryice.ai/products-and-platforms/lucy

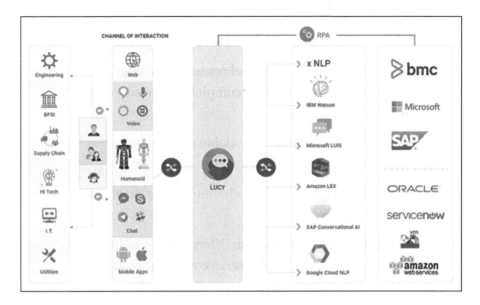

Figure 3-3. *Lucy architectural overview*

- **Channel of interaction:** Converses with users in the medium of choice. It supports web, voice, chat, mobile apps, and humanoids.

- **Natural language processing (NLP):** Leverages any existing NLP engine based on the enterprise requirements. It uses NLP to interpret the intent of the user by comprehending the meaning, determining the appropriate action, and responding to users.

- **Enterprise integration:** Integrates with multiple enterprise systems and knowledge sources so that users can rely on Lucy as a single source of information from disparate sources.

- **Enterprise-grade security:** Provides data region flexibility with endpoint-based security and third-party integrations. The current version of Lucy is SAML and SSO-enabled.

- **Flexible billing:** Offers a custom-fit billing model with numerous billing templates and usage categories.

- **Context Switching:** Multilevel context switching allows users to get back to incomplete conversations or digressed conversation.

- **On-demand scalability:** A scalable platform for a business's needs.

- **Omnichannel:** Various OTB channels are available to easily configure.

- **OTB third-party integration:** Offers out-of-the-box third-party integration with service management, robotic process automation, and CRM providers.

- **Configuration management:** As a cognitive virtual assistant, Lucy can act as an interface between the users and multiple enterprise applications across domains and business functions.

- **Platform agnostic:** Works across platforms, including Skype, Facebook Messenger, Microsoft Teams, Slack, and many more.

Conclusion

This chapter overviewed various bot frameworks that a developer can chose from to rapidly create cognitive bot applications by integrating with cognitive platforms.

CHAPTER 4

Building Your First Bot Using Watson Assistant

Watson Assistant is a cognitive cloud service offering by IBM that makes it easier for developers to build conversational interfaces and embed them into any application. Watson Assistant integrates with a variety of cognitive services provided by the IBM Watson platform to enrich the conversation through spell checks, a tone analyzer, and other services.

Watson Assistant is easily integrated with popular messaging platforms like Facebook Messenger and Slack. Developers also have the option to create a custom user interface application and work with configured workflows through APIs.

Let's go through the steps of creating a simple CVA. Let's start with the creation of an IBM Cloud account using which we will be consuming the Watson Assistant Services.

Creation of an IBM Cloud Account

Navigate to `https://cloud.ibm.com/registration` to sign up for an IBM Cloud account. Figure 4-1 shows the IBM Cloud account sign-up page.

© Navin Sabharwal, Sudipta Barua, Neha Anand, Pallavi Aggarwal 2020
N. Sabharwal et al., *Developing Cognitive Bots Using the IBM Watson Engine*,
https://doi.org/10.1007/978-1-4842-5555-1_4

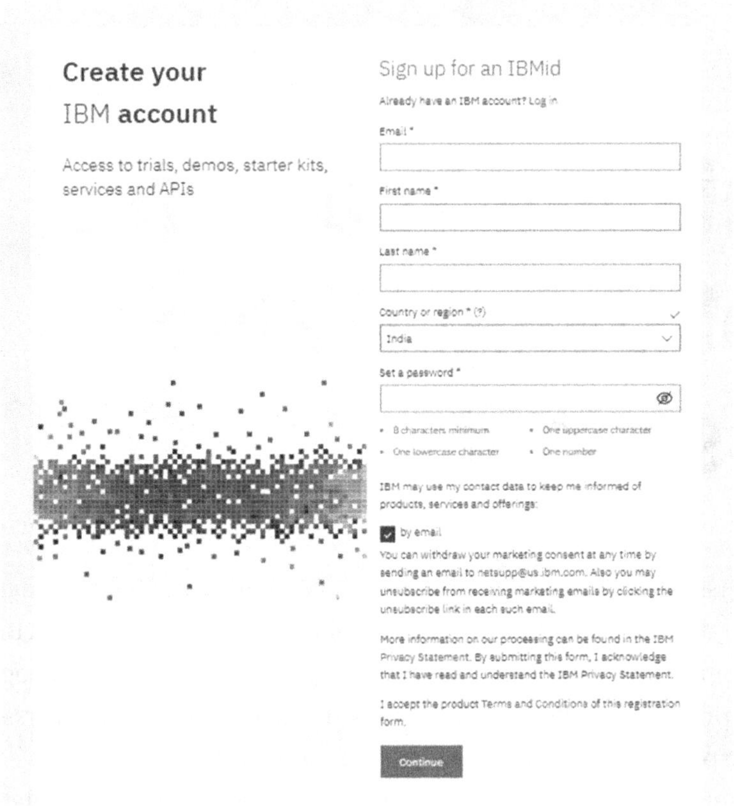

Figure 4-1.   *IBM Cloud account sign-up*

Enter the required information, as shown in Figure 4-2, and click **Continue**.

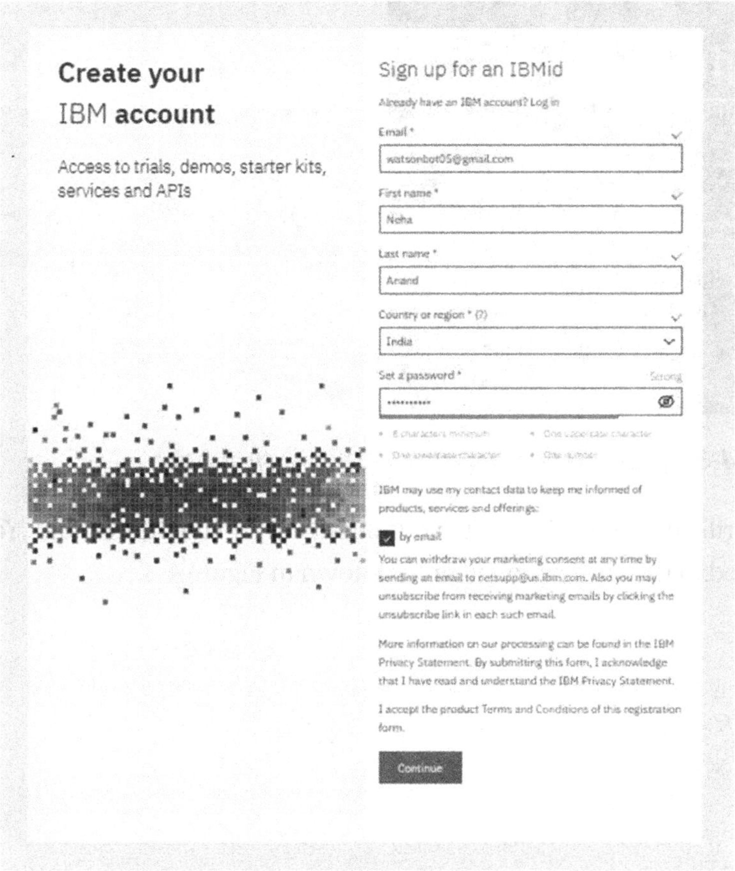

Figure 4-2. *Sign-up page with information entered*

This takes you to the screen shown in Figure 4-3, which is a confirmation page. It confirms the association of the email ID with an IBM account. Click **Create Account**.

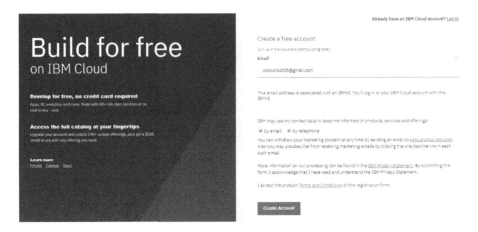

Figure 4-3. *Email ID association confirmation page*

A verification code is sent to your email to validate the account. You are redirected to the verification page, as shown in Figure 4-4.

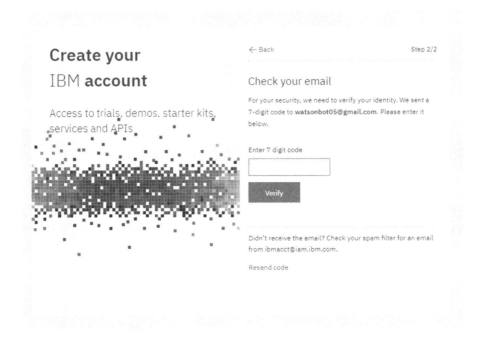

Figure 4-4. *Account verification page*

Enter the verification code that you received and click **Verify**, as shown in Figure 4-5.

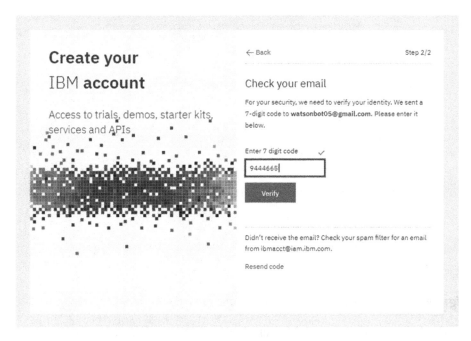

Figure 4-5. *Verification page with code*

Post verification, you are redirected to the IBM Cloud account privacy page, as shown in Figure 4-6.

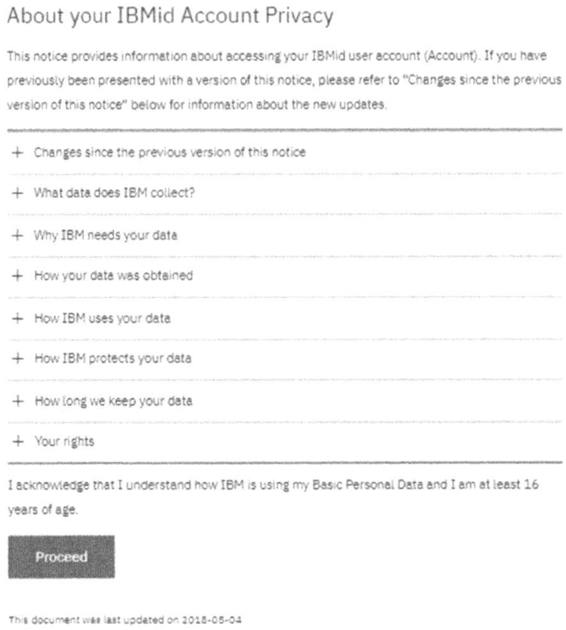

About your IBMid Account Privacy
This notice provides information about accessing your IBMid user account (Account). If you have previously been presented with a version of this notice, please refer to "Changes since the previous version of this notice" below for information about the new updates.
+ Changes since the previous version of this notice
+ What data does IBM collect?
+ Why IBM needs your data
+ How your data was obtained
+ How IBM uses your data
+ How IBM protects your data
+ How long we keep your data
+ Your rights
I acknowledge that I understand how IBM is using my Basic Personal Data and I am at least 16 years of age.
Proceed
This document was last updated on 2018-05-04

***Figure 4-6.** IBM account privacy page*

Click **Proceed**. You are redirected to the IBM Product Space page, as shown in Figure 4-7.

You are on the US site. Would you like to switch to a localized version?
Yes
No thanks
IBM
Search
My IBM
Profile
Billing
IBMid: watsonbot05@gmail.com
Neha, your IBM product space is ready!
Need help? Get support
Get started today with an IBM product purchase or free trial.
Start filling your IBM products page with offerings that will solve your technology and business needs. Free trials available.
View catalog
Let's talk
Contact IBM
Privacy
Terms of use
Accessibility
Feedback
United States - English

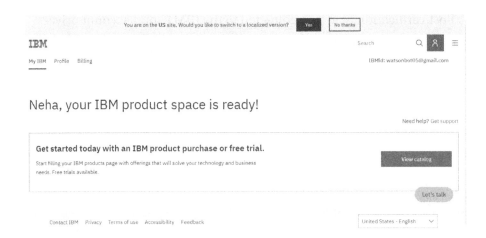

***Figure 4-7.** IBM Product Space page*

Click **View catalog**. This takes you to the page shown in Figure 4-8, which enables you to start the free 30-day trial. Click **Free 30-day trial**.

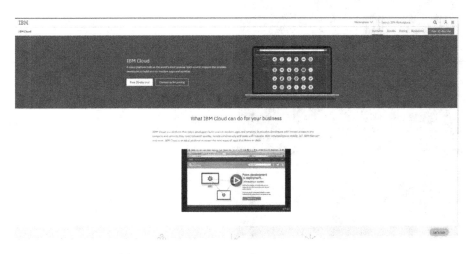

Figure 4-8. *Enable Free 30-Day Trial*

This takes you to the page shown in Figure 4-9. Click **Start your Free Trial**.

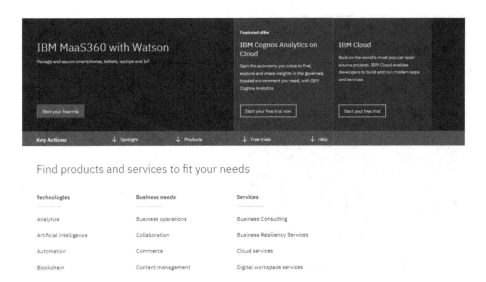

Figure 4-9. *Start your free trial*

53

You are redirected to the Login page, as shown in Figure 4-10.

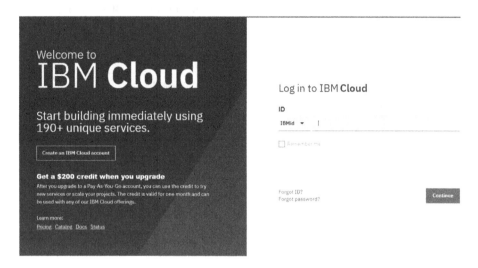

Figure 4-10. *IBM Cloud login page*

Here you need to specify the email ID that you registered earlier. Enter this information and click **Log in** (see Figure 4-11).

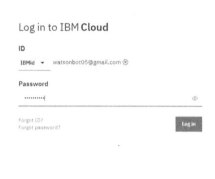

Figure 4-11. *Login information*

You are asked to confirm your account and accept the Terms of Use, as shown in Figure 4-12.

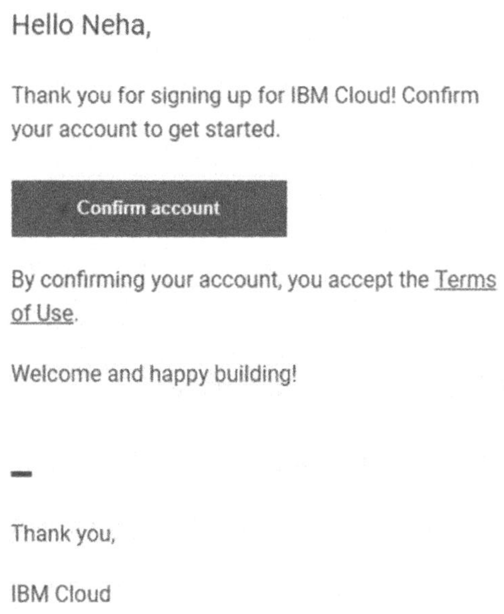

Hello Neha,

Thank you for signing up for IBM Cloud! Confirm your account to get started.

Confirm account

By confirming your account, you accept the Terms of Use.

Welcome and happy building!

—

Thank you,

IBM Cloud

Figure 4-12. *Confirm account*

Click **Confirm account**. With this confirmation, your account is set up. Log in again and you're redirected to the IBM Cloud Dashboard page, as shown in Figure 4-13.

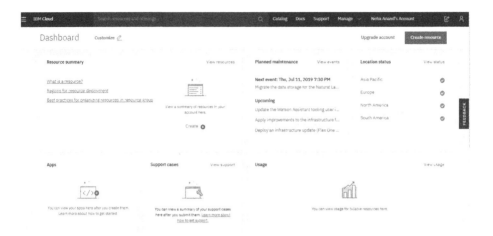

Figure 4-13. *IBM Cloud Dashboard page*

The Dashboard page includes important information.

- A summary of the resources that you are consuming

- The status of IBM Cloud services at various geographies

- The planned maintenance schedule

- Resource usage

Spend some time on the Dashboard page to become familiar with the interface.

Creating the Watson Assistant Service

To start the bot creation, you need to search for the service that we plan to use in the catalog, which is the Watson Assistant service.

You can search in the catalog for the **Watson Assistant** service, as shown in Figure 4-14, or you can click **AI** in the **All Categories** section, as shown in Figure 4-15.

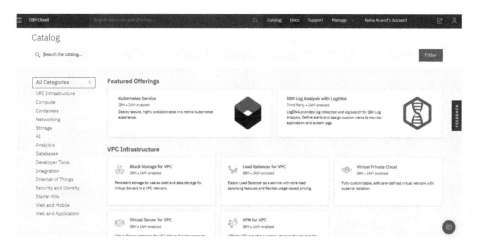

Figure 4-14. *IBM Cloud Catalog page*

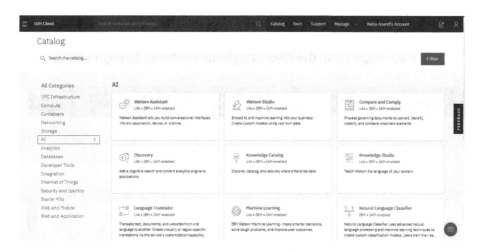

Figure 4-15. *IBM Cloud AI Category page*

From here, you can select the **Watson Assistant** service. Enter the required information to create the service. Give the service a name, which should reflect the cognitive virtual assistant service that you want to create.

In this example, we have simply named it Watson Assistant-BFSI, as shown in Figure 4-16, to reflect the use case.

Select the region where you want to deploy this resource. Keep the resource group set at the default, which is London in this example.

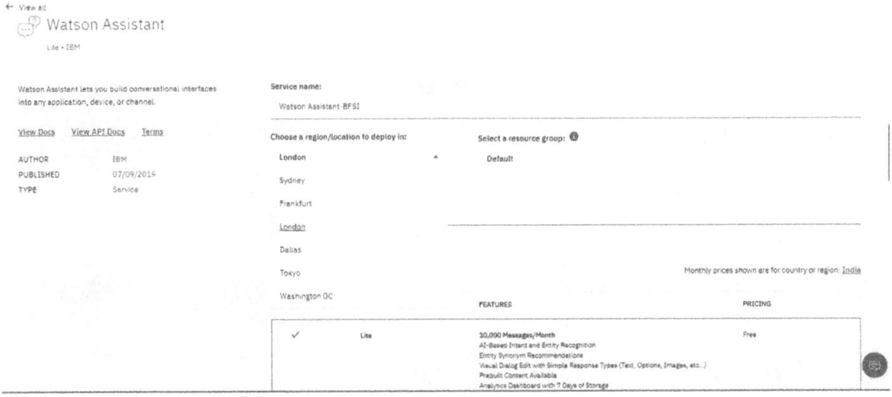

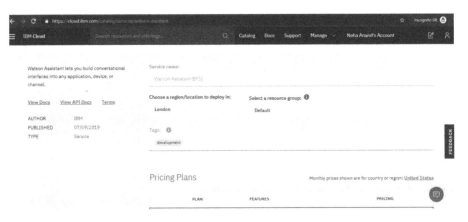

Figure 4-16. *Watson Assistant Service create page*

Define the region and the resource group, as shown in Figure 4-17.

Figure 4-17. *Watson Assistant Service Region selection page*

The wizard screen prompts you to choose the plan for this service, as shown in Figure 4-18. Since it is a trial account, let's use the Lite plan, which is free but has limits on consumption. You can review the features of the plan on this page.

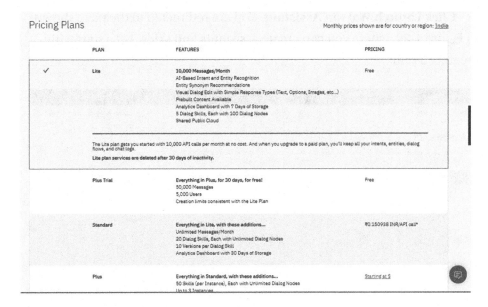

Figure 4-18. *IBM Cloud AI Category page*

After making the plan selection, click **Create**.

The service is created, and the resource list page shows you the parameters, including the API key and URL, as shown in Figure 4-19.

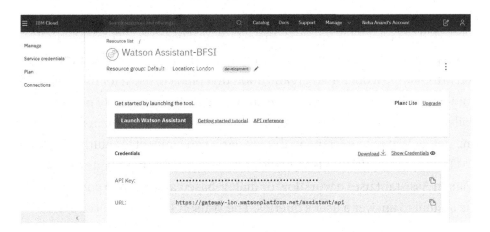

Figure 4-19. *Watson Assistant service page*

Click **Launch Watson Assistant**. You are redirected to the page shown in Figure 4-20, where you can create assistants and skills. Let's start with creating a skill.

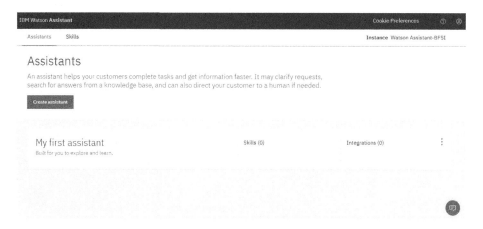

Figure 4-20. *Watson Assistants page*

Creating a Skill for the Use Cases

Before proceeding with the skill creation, let's take a deep dive into what a skill is and how it is used to create a bot.

A skill is a container for a specific category of use cases. Think of a skill as a repository of use cases that belong to specific domain. For example, if you are creating a bot for an organization that plans to use it for multiple domains—like HR, finance, end consumers, and IT— you create multiple skills. The bot is able to answer queries across all of these domains. Thus, one bot, or Watson Assistant, in this scenario can connect to multiple skills.

There are two IBM Watson services that respond to users' questions. Watson Assistant uses a workflow or dialog-based approach to configure the system to answer a user's queries. The Watson Discovery service uses a search-and-extract method to answer user queries and return matching documents. We cover the Watson Assistant service first to configure our bot, and then provide an overview and integration of the Watson Discovery service.

Corresponding to the two services, there are two types of skills that you can create in Watson.

- **Dialog skill:** This corresponds to the Watson Assistant service. It contains the dialog workflow, which is a step-by-step process on how the conversation flows between the user asking the questions and the Watson assistant responding to them. It also contains intents and entities, which are the backbone of Watson's cognitive capabilities. They help the bot understand the intent of the user and the object of the conversation. We train the system using a variation of questions that a user may ask; this is part of the skill.

- **Search skill:** This corresponds to the Watson Discovery service to search and extract relevant information from a document repository.

Let's start by exploring the Skills section. We'll create a simple skill and attach it to the Watson Assistant. Click **Skills** and then click **Create Skill**, as shown in Figure 4-21.

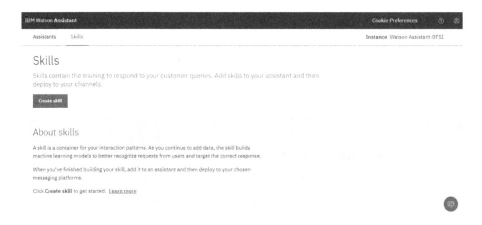

Figure 4-21. *Watson Assistant skill page*

The Create Skill page has two options: the Dialog skill and the Search skill, as shown in Figure 4-22. Select **Dialog skill** and click **Next**.

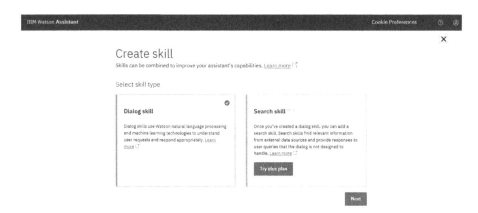

Figure 4-22. *Watson Assistant Create Skill page*

This takes you to the Create Dialog Skill page, as shown in Figure 4-23. There are three options.

- **Create skill:** A custom skill that is created from scratch.

- **Use sample skill:** Watson-provided sample skills that for learning or test purposes.

- **Import skill:** You can import the JSON of a previously created skill.

We are creating the skill from scratch, so we'll use the first option and enter the required information. Provide a name and a brief description of the skill. Choose your language and click **Create dialog skill**.

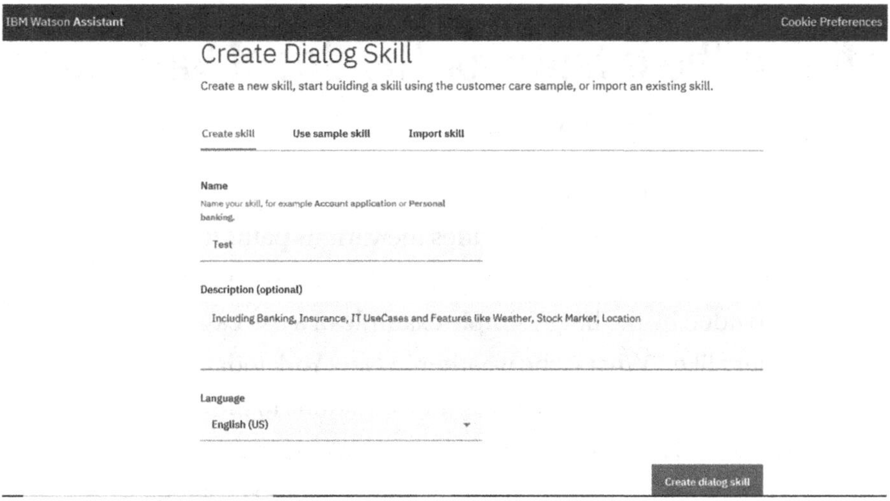

Figure 4-23. *Dialog Skill information*

The Skills workspace page is shown in Figure 4-24. It has the required options: Intents, Entities, and Dialog. Let's work with them to create our first skill and attach it to the Watson Assistant bot.

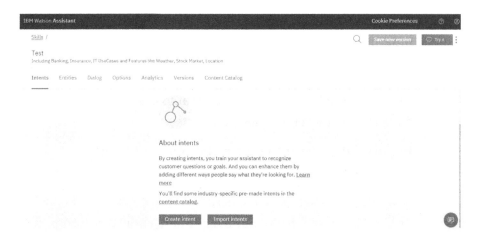

Figure 4-24. *Skill workspace page*

Defining the Intents for the Set of Variations

Let's first review some of the key terms.

- **Use case:** A use case is a scenario or a query initiated by the user. The use case includes the various paths that a conversation can take and the end response that is provided by the bot. A simple example of a use case is a query like, "What is the weather in New York today?" The bot uses the intents, entities, and variations to provide the answer to this query. A complex use case scenario is an IT helpdesk and a user trying to solve a laptop problem.

- **Intent:** The verb or action in the conversation with the user. The cognitive virtual assistant tries to understand the core intent or verb from the conversation with the user. For example, the intent of a user query such as *"Tell me about the insurance policy?"* would be *"enquire"* since the user wants to enquire or gather information. In this scenario, the object is *"insurance policy."*

- **Entities:** Entities are the nouns that combine with the intent to identify particular action. In the preceding example, the entity is "insurance policy." This is a simplistic explanation of an entity; we will delve deeper into entities and how to define and configure them in Watson.

- **System entities:** Predefined entities provided by Watson are called system entities; for example, *@sys-currency, @sys-date, @sys-location, @sys-time,* and so forth. A complete listing is shown in Figure 4-25. To use these entities, we need to enable them, so check the On status for the specific system entities that you want to use.

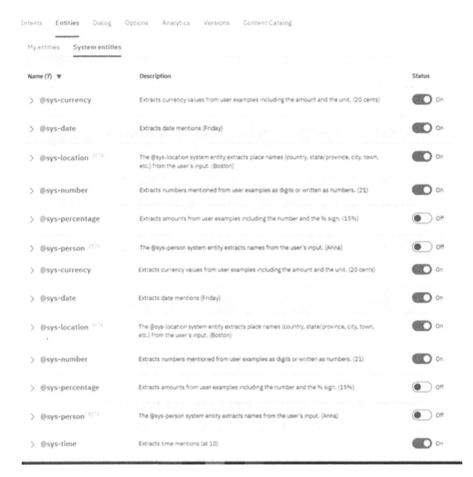

Figure 4-25. *System entities*

- **Patterns entities:** Watson provides a feature of defining regular expressions in entity values. These entities are useful when we are supposed to identify defined patterns, such as a telephone number, credit card number, ticket numbers, and so forth. For example, if you want to define a regular expression for a standard US phone number, it supports the following formats.

```
###-###-####
(###) ###-####
### ### ####
###.###.####
```

We can define this regular expression as **^(\+\d{1,2}\s)?\(?\d{3}\)?**
[\s.-]\d{3}[\s.-]\d{4}$ in the Pattern section of the entity value, as shown
in Figure 4-26.

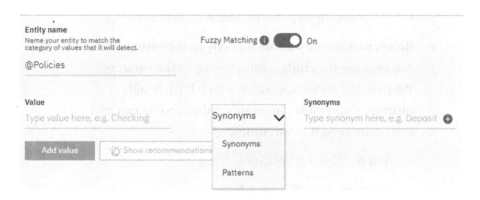

Figure 4-26. *Pattern selection for entity*

- **Variations:** Variations are a set of sample utterances
  from a set of end users in the use case that we are
  defining. This is an ideal scenario in which we get
  actual data on how the end users frame their questions.
  This sample data from multiple users trains the IBM
  Watson engine so that it can learn to map the query
  from users to the intent.

- **Referencing entity values and synonyms in the intent**
  variations: Since we are defining the entities and values
  related to the variations, we can add entity values or
  synonyms in the variations to have a relation mapping
  between the intents and entities. In the preceding

example, we want to add the variations related to the insurance policies. We have the *@Policies* entity with values such as health insurance and motor insurance, so we can add these values as part of the variations. The following are examples of such variations.

- Tell me about health insurance policy.

- What is the motor insurance policy?

- What are the benefits of health insurance?

- **Referencing entity name directly in the intent:** We can also use the entity name directly in the variations. We have the @Policies entity, which have health insurance and motor insurance values, so we can add this entity as part of variations.

  - Tell me about @Policies

  - What are the different @Policies

  - Help me with the information about @Policies

- **Testing the intents:** After defining the intents and variations, we can test it in Watson's ***Try it*** panel on the right side of the Skill page, as shown in Figure 4-27. You can see the intent triggered based on the variations added.

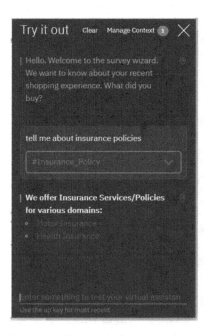

Figure 4-27. *Try It Out panel on Dialog page*

This way, you can check whether the intent triggered is correct or not. If not, then we can retrain the system by selecting the correct intent from the drop-down list. The Watson engine takes a moment to retrain and shows "Watson Training" in the Try It Out panel. Once the training is complete, you can test our intent again and see that Watson returns the correct response, as shown in Figure 4-28.

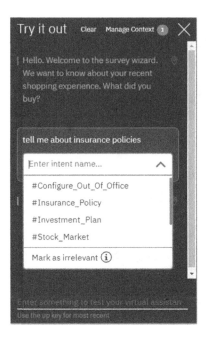

Figure 4-28. *Try It Out panel on Dialog page and Intents drop-down list*

You can also edit, rename, delete, add, or move any intent from Intent page, where all the intents are listed. You can also export and import intents

- **Export:** Selects the intent page. You can select the intents that you want to export and click **Export**. The intents selected are downloaded in a CSV file, which is useful if you want to reuse the intents in another skill.

- **Import:** If you want to add intents and variations, then you can do it by uploading a CSV file in the **<example>,<intent>** format, where the example is the variation for a particular intent (see Table 4-1). The structure of the CSV file should be as follows in the example.

- Tell me about health insurance policy, Insurance_Policy

- What is the motor insurance policy, Insurance_Policy

- What are the benefits of health insurance, Insurance_Policy

There is an import option on the Intents page. Click it to import.

It is useful when you have a large training set that you can create offline and then import into the Watson skill.

- **Dialog:** A dialog is a flow or a tree structure that defines the workflow for a conversation. A dialog is a step-by-step process through which we try to understand the user's intent. The dialog uses intents, entities, and webhooks to integrate with third-party APIs or systems for fetching data.

Table 4-1. *Use Case and Variations*

Use Case	Variations
Insurance Policy	Tell me about insurance policies.
Insurance Policy	What other insurance services are there?
Insurance Policy	I want to know about various insurance policies.
Insurance Policy	What other insurance services are there?
Insurance Policy	Tell me about motor insurance.
Insurance Policy	What are the benefits of health insurance policy?
Insurance Policy	What are the features of the motor insurance policy?
Insurance Policy	What is motor insurance?
Insurance Policy	Tell me about different types of insurance policies.
Insurance Policy	Tell me the benefits of motor insurance.

Now that we have explained the basics of what goes into training the bot, let's create a use case in a step-by-step fashion.

The first step is to identify the use case; for this example, it is from the insurance sector. The user wants to find out the types of insurance policies available from your company.

It is practical to document everything in a spreadsheet before you start making changes to the IBM Watson configurations.

- **Intent Description:** The types of policies available from a provider.

- **Intent Name:** #Insurance_Policy

- **Entity:** Insurance policy types

- **Entity Values:** Health Insurance, Motor Insurance

Next, we need utterances or variations from end users on how they might ask for this information.

- Insurance services

- Tell me about insurance policies

- What other insurance services are there?

- I want to know about various insurance policies.

Let's now move to the IBM Watson console to configure our first use case.

1. After logging in to IBM Cloud, launch the AI service created earlier in the chapter: Watson Assistant – Virtual Bot.

2. Click **Skills** and then select the Test skill.

3. In the top menu bar, select **Intent**. The intent is named with a # sign followed by the name of the intent. We will call our intent #Insurance_Policy.

4. Enter a brief description of the intent that you are creating. The **Add user example** option appears.

5. Enter the variations defined earlier, as shown in Figure 4-29. These are the sample variations that are fed into the Watson engine for training.

Figure 4-29. *Intent page for adding the variations*

Add at least five examples/variations as intent examples. A higher number of variations is better for training purposes, which results in better responses from the bot.

As a best practice and for the engine to have enough data, you should have 20 to 50 unique variations for each intent.

After entering the variations, the screen looks as it is shown in Figure 4-30.

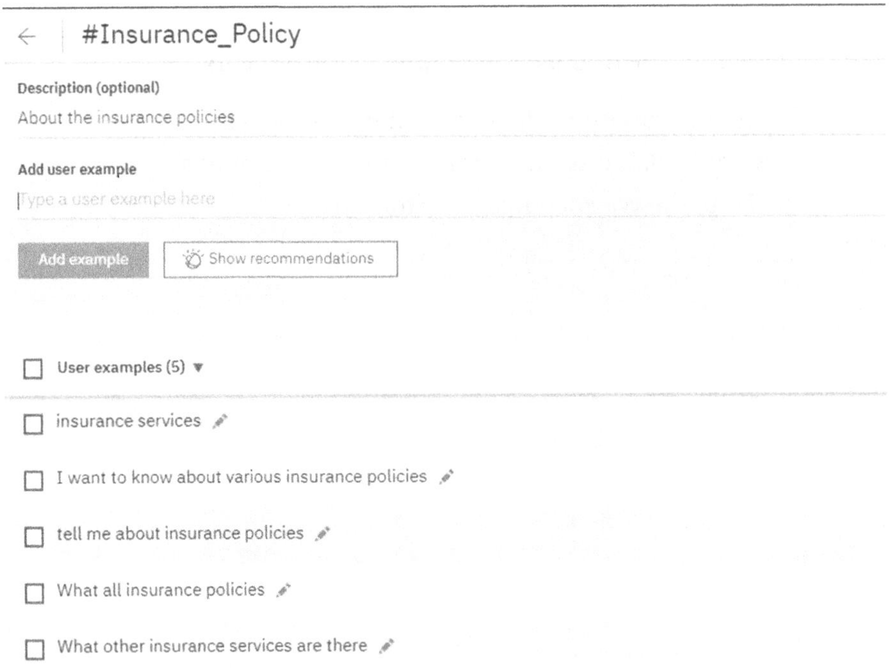

← | #Insurance_Policy

Description (optional)
About the insurance policies

Add user example
Type a user example here

[Add example]   [☼ Show recommendations]

☐ User examples (5) ▼

☐ insurance services 🖉

☐ I want to know about various insurance policies 🖉

☐ tell me about insurance policies 🖉

☐ What all insurance policies 🖉

☐ What other insurance services are there 🖉

Figure 4-30. *Intent page with variations added*

We are done configuring the intent and its variations, but we still haven't configured the entities for the system to decipher what the user wants.

1. Click the **Back** button to go back to the Skill page.

2. Select **Entities** from the top menu. You are presented with a screen, as shown in Figure 4-31.

3. Enter @Policies in Entity name. For the values, add Motor Insurance with Motor Insurance. Add Health Insurance with Health Insurance as the synonym.

4. Turn **Fuzzy Matching** on if you want to autodiscover synonyms by using the built-in fuzzy logic algorithms provided by Watson. This enables better matching of entity values by relying on built-in libraries and data available within the engine.

Figure 4-31. Entity page

After completing the configuration of the entities, intents, and variations, we need to tie down all using a dialog. In Watson Assistant, a dialog is represented graphically as a tree structure in which you can create a node to process each intent.

Dialog Configuration

Let's configure our dialog flow and then dive into it.

1. Click the **Back** button to go the Dialog page.

2. On the Dialog page, click the hamburger menu on the Welcome node (this node is created by default), as depicted in Figure 4-32.

Figure 4-32. Hamburger menu on a node

3. Select **Add node below**, as shown in Figure 4-33.

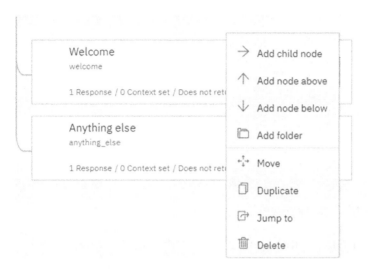

Figure 4-33. *Add node below*

A node is added below the Welcome node, as shown in Figure 4-34.

Figure 4-34. *Node added*

4. Click the newly added node and name it **Insurance Policy**, as shown in Figure 4-35.

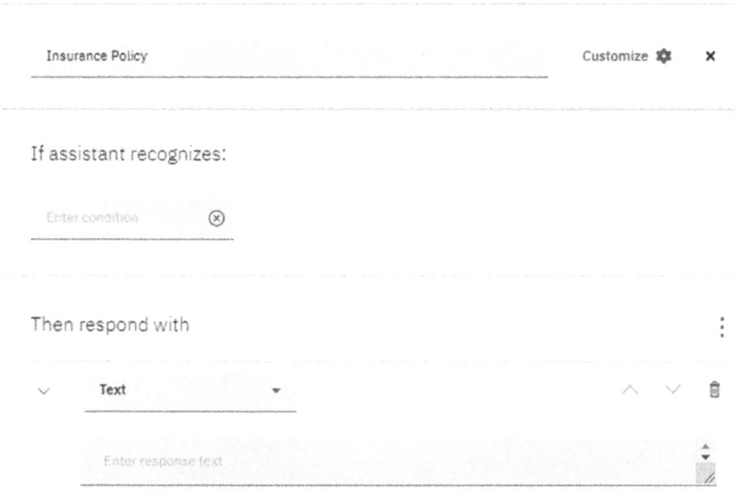

Insurance Policy   Customize ⚙   ✕

If assistant recognizes:

Enter condition   ⊗

Then respond with   ⋮

⌄   Text   ▾   ∧   ⌄   🗑

Enter response text

Figure 4-35. *Node name entered*

5. In the **Enter condition** field, provide the intent
    that you have created (i.e., **#Insurance_Policy**), as
    shown in Figure 4-36.

Figure 4-36. *Dialog node with intent defined in the condition*

6. In the **Then respond with** field, provide the
    response that you want to show when the condition
    is matched. The response field shows **Enter
    response text**, so we'll add the response to show in
    our bot (see Figure 4-37).

Figure 4-37. *Option selected from the Then respond with field drop-down*

7. There are two options: Health Insurance and Motor Insurance. In the **Then respond with** drop-down menu, select **Option**, as shown in Figure 4-38 and Figure 4-39.

Figure 4-38. *Option selected*

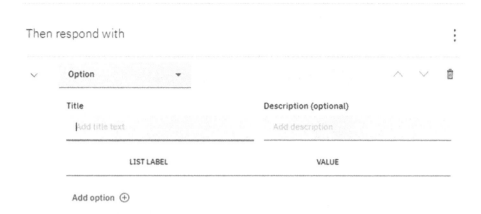

Figure 4-39. *Option selected from Then respond with*

8. In the Title field, add a statement and a description for the option, as shown in Figure 4-40.

Figure 4-40. *Title and description*

9. Click **Add option** to add the different types of policies (i.e., Motor Insurance and Health Insurance). Add these in the List Label with Value, as shown in Figure 4-41. These are the values defined in the @Policies entity.

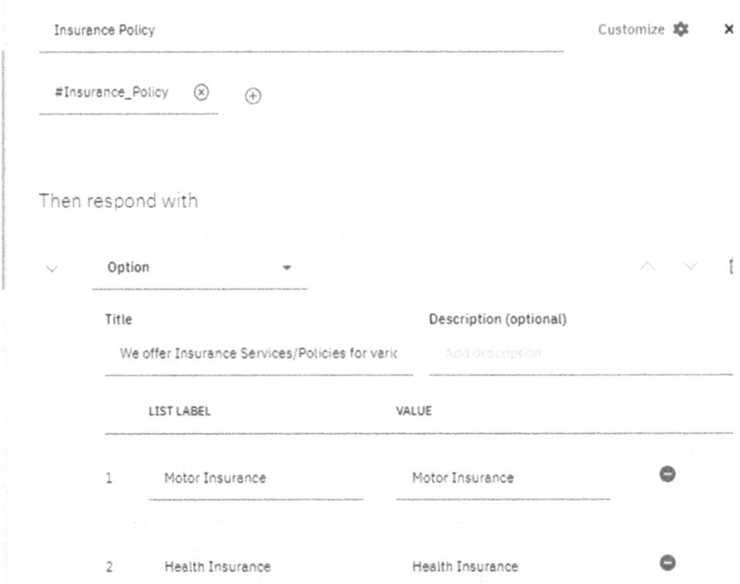

Figure 4-41. *Dialog node defining Response field giving options*

10. The options that we'll be showing to the user will
     be defined as entity and values. As in this case,
     @Policies will be the entity with values defined as
     Motor Insurance and Health Insurance with their
     respective synonyms.

11. You have defined the options in the node, now
     return to the node. Click the hamburger menu and
     select **Add child node**, as shown in Figure 4-42.
     Since we have two options, add two child nodes.

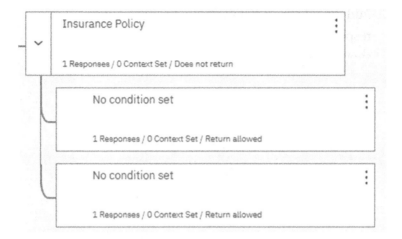

Figure 4-42. *Child nodes added for options defined*

12. Define the conditions in the child nodes as their entity and entity value. For example, @Policies:(Motor Insurance) and @Policies:(Health Insurance) are defined as the options. We are adding two nodes for the two options, as shown in Figure 4-43.

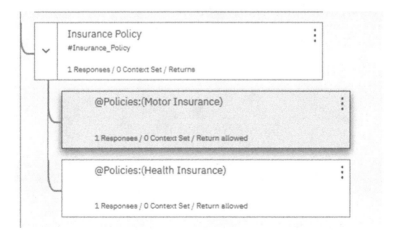

Figure 4-43. *Child nodes with conditions defined as their entity values*

13. Add the response that you want to show in the response field when any option is selected, as shown in Figure 4-44.

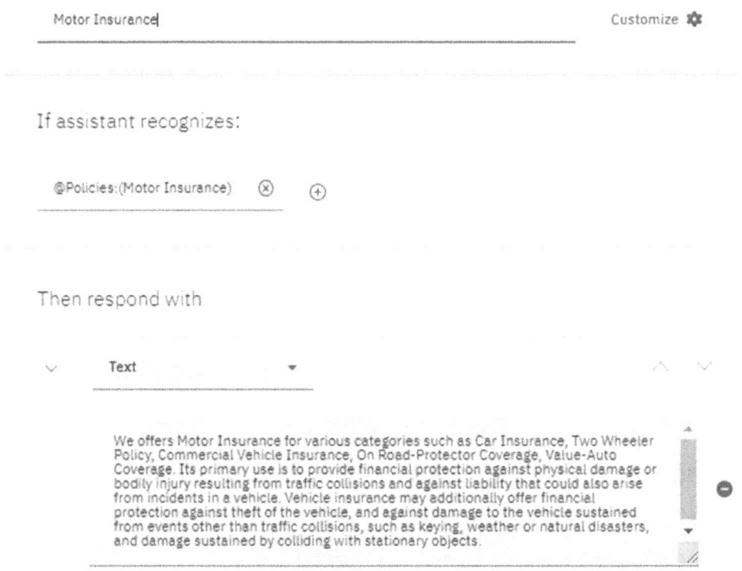

Figure 4-44. *Child node with response*

Let's try out our use case on the Watson console (i.e., Try It Out panel). Click **Try it out** in the Dialog page. You are presented with a welcome message, and you can chat with the bot. Type a query to check the response, as shown in Figure 4-45 and Figure 4-46.

Figure 4-45. *Try It Out panel to test the use case*

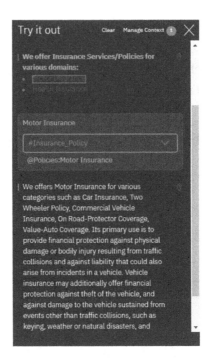

Figure 4-46. *The response to the selected option*

Wow! That's all there is to creating and testing your first cognitive bot. Next, let's integrate the skill with Watson's built-in bot framework assistant to complete the configuration.

Integrating with the Built-in Bot Framework Assistant

Watson offers a built-in bot called an *assistant* to link our skill/dialog. Select **Assistants**, and click **Create assistant**, as shown in Figure 4-47.

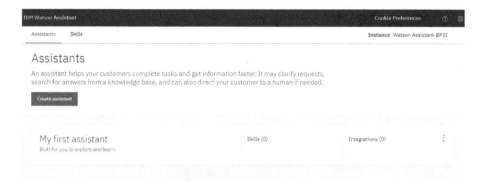

Figure 4-47. *Creating Assistant page*

Name the chatbot that you are creating and enter the required information. Click **Enable Preview Link** and **Create assistant**, as shown in Figure 4-48.

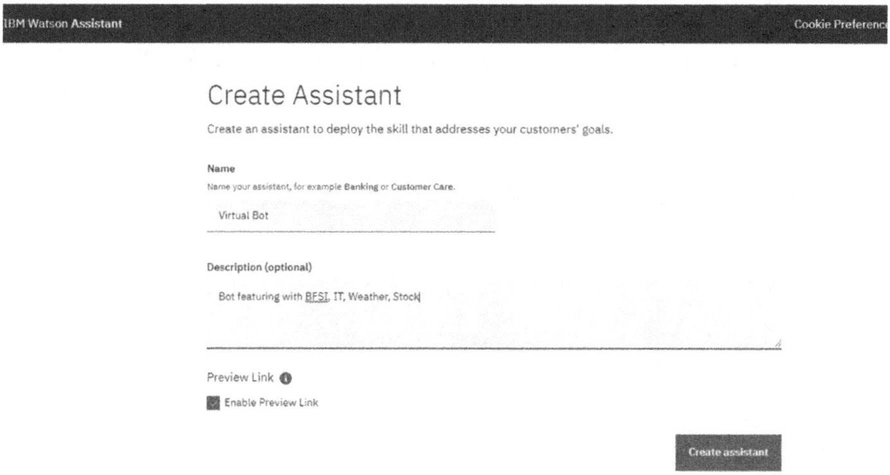

Figure 4-48. *Name the assistant and create it*

Click **Add dialog skill**, as shown in Figure 4-49. Select and add the skill that you have created, as shown in Figure 4-50.

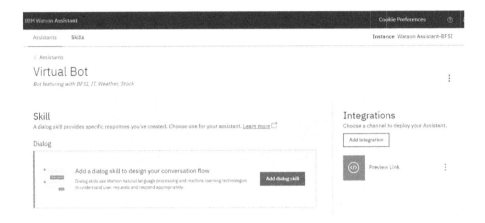

Figure 4-49. *Add Dialog skill to your assistant*

Figure 4-50. *Select the skill to be added to the assistant*

Select the skill and the assistant linked via the Preview link. Click the
Test Skill. You see it selected, as shown in Figure 4-51.

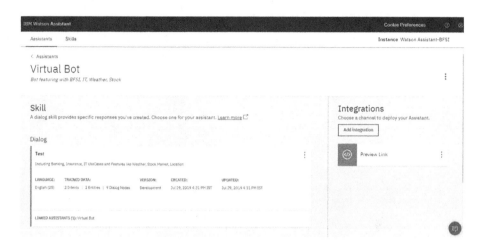

Figure 4-51. *Preview link created on Assistant page*

Your First Bot

Click the **Preview Link**. Your chatbot link opens in a new tab, as shown in
Figure 4-52.

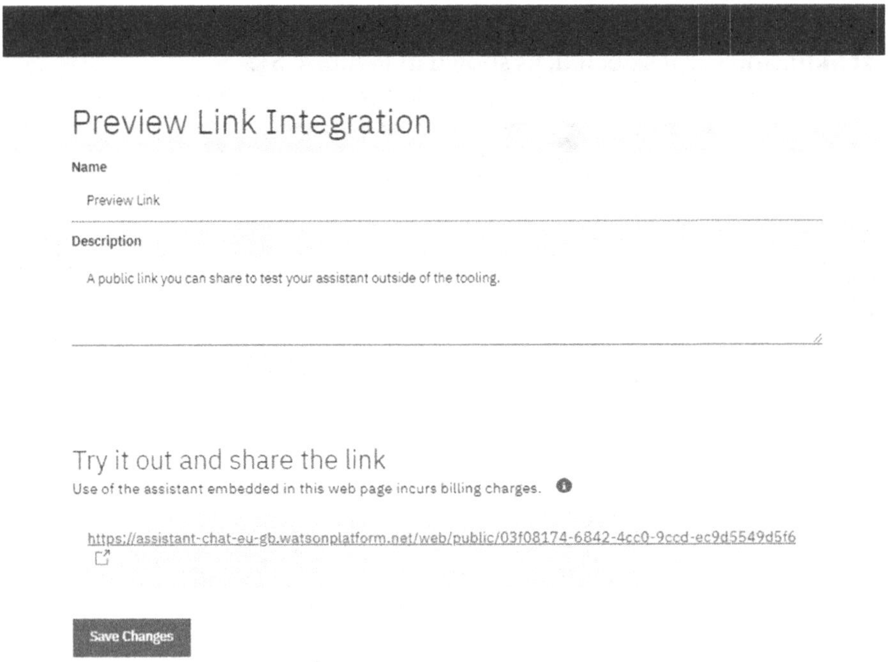

Figure 4-52. *Select Preview Link to see the bot*

You can see the bot in the tab after selecting the Preview link, as shown in Figure 4-53.

Figure 4-53. *Preview bot provided by Watson*

Now you can try out the use case on your bot and see the results, as shown in Figure 4-54.

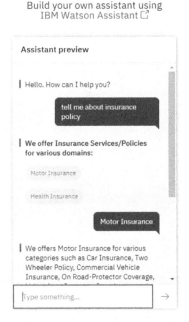

Figure 4-54. *Trying on the bot*

Dialog and Conditions

Dialog Node

A dialog node contains a condition and a response.

- Condition: The information or check required to trigger a particular dialog node. It can be an intent, an entity, a combination of intents and entities, entity values, or a context variable. There are also predefined conditions by Watson that can be used; for example, true, false, welcome, anything_else, conversation_start, and so on.

- Response: The response mentioned in the response
  field of a node; it executes when the condition is true.

Single Node

A single node can handle simple user queries (i.e., a simple question and answer). But real-life use cases are more complex; there is a to-and-fro communication between the bot and the user. You can use multiple nodes in the same hierarchy. You can also use child nodes to create a workflow.

Watson processes or traverses all nodes in a top-down approach in the tree. It starts with the first node and traverses until the last node.

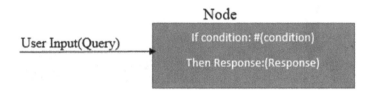

Figure 4-55. *Single node representation*

Multiple Nodes

When traversing the nodes, if the condition matches, it enters/triggers the node and executes the workflow. It executes each of the child nodes until the condition is met.

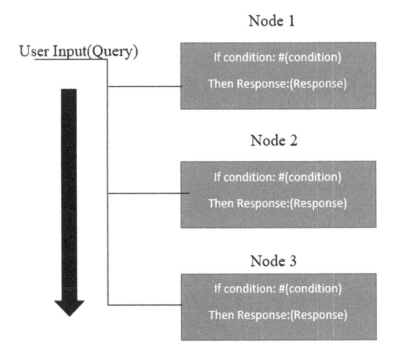

Figure 4-56. *Traversing among Multiple nodes*

Node with Child Nodes

Let's say that the user's query matches the condition in Node 2. It triggers Node 2 while traversing from Node 1, and then it evaluates the child nodes (Child Node 1, Child 2). Whichever child node's condition is met executes that particular child node. After that will come out of the child node workflow and continues moving downward until the last node in the parent branch (i.e., Node 3).

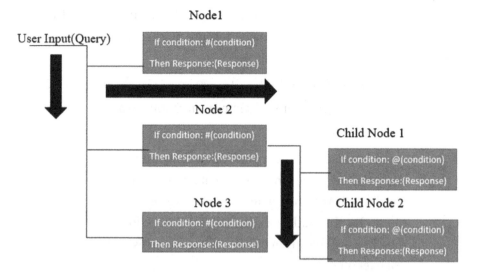

Figure 4-57. *Traversing among node with child nodes*

Now that you have learned how the dialog is used, let's look at the various options available. On the Dialog page, click **Create dialog**, as shown in Figure 4-58.

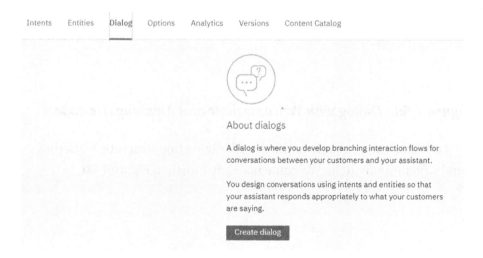

Figure 4-58. *Dialog page to create a dialog*

By default, the dialog has two nodes named Welcome and Anything else, as shown in Figure 4-59. These names are not fixed, and you can modify them.

- Welcome node: The bot's welcome message, which is displayed to the user when she starts a conversation with the bot.

- Anything else node: A special node that comes with the welcome node when you create a dialog. If no condition is matched in any of the nodes in the hierarchy, this node is executed. If the workflow matches the condition of any other node, this node is not executed.

Figure 4-59. *Dialog with Welcome node and Anything else node*

Let's add another node to the default dialog tree structure. Click the hamburger menu on the Welcome node, as shown in Figure 4-60.

Figure 4-60. *Hamburger menu on a node*

Click **Add node below**, as shown in Figure 4-61.

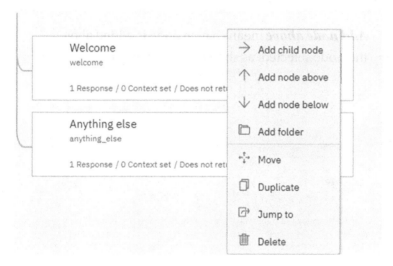

Figure 4-61. *Add a node option for a particular node*

The options on the pop-up menu are simple and self-explanatory, but let's brief describe these options. **Add child node** adds a node as a child to the same, as shown in Figure 4-62. We will use the child node in this example.

Figure 4-62. *Add child node*

Add node above means a new node is added above
the node selected, as shown in Figure 4-63.

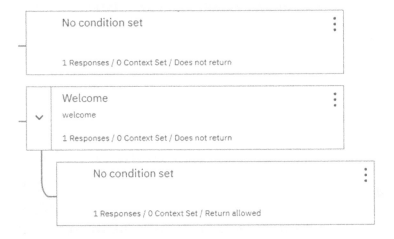

Figure 4-63. *Add node above*

Add node below means a new node is added below
the node selected, as shown in Figure 4-64.

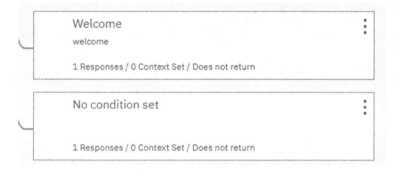

Figure 4-64. *Add node below*

Add folder adds a folder. Folders help you organize
sections of your tree around similar use cases. To
get started, move the existing dialog nodes into this
folder or add new nodes directly into your folder, as
shown in Figure 4-65. Folder names can be based on
the domains for which you have multiple dialogs.

Figure 4-65. *Add folder*

Move means a node can be moved as a child node,
above another node, or below another node, as
shown in Figure 4-66.

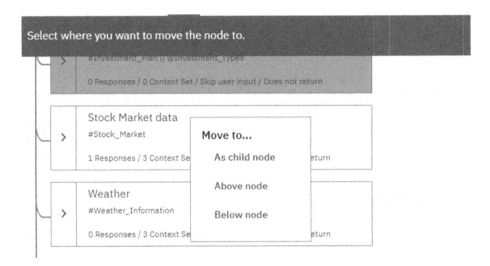

Figure 4-66. *Move option to move a node to another node*

> *Duplicate* creates a clone/duplicate/copy of the
> same node as shown in Figure 4-67

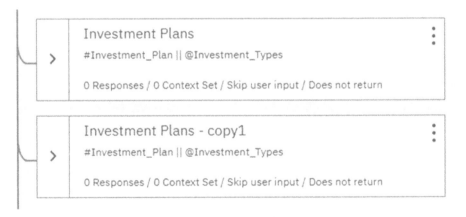

Figure 4-67. *Duplicate a node*

Delete deletes the node.

Skip user input is used when you want to bypass waiting for user input and go directly to the first child node of the current node. It is enabled if a node has one or more child nodes.

Jump to is a condition statement that provides an option to create branches and jump from one node to another node in the workflow if certain conditions are met. You need to select the node from which you want to jump. Select the node where you want to jump to in the workflow, and then configure one of the three options, as shown in Figure 4-68.

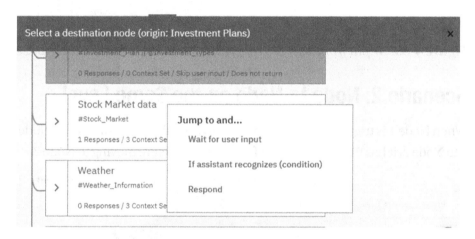

Figure 4-68. *Jump To option*

Wait for user input waits for the user to input the query, and then it moves the workflow to the next step. The dialog will not progress until the user provides more input.

Scenario 1: Node with Child Nodes

When a user enters a query, it triggers the matched node and waits for the user to input something. If that user input is matched with the condition defined in the subsequent child nodes (Child Node 1, Child Node 2), it executes that particular child node.

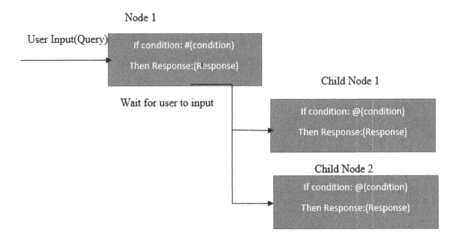

Figure 4-69. *Input from user & Traversal from main Node to child Nodes*

Scenario 2: Node to Node on the Same Level

When Node 1 is triggered on a matched query, and there is a jump from Node 1 to Node 2, it has the option to wait for user input before moving to Node 2.

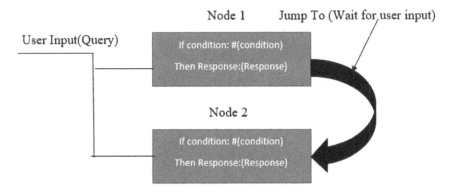

Figure 4-70. *Input from user & Traversal from Node to Node on the same level*

If bot recognizes condition means that if the condition specified in the target node evaluates to true, the workflow executes the response statement of the target node. If it does not evaluate to true, the response statement is not executed.

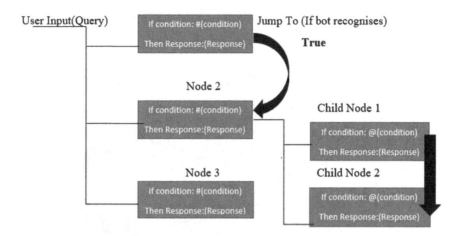

Figure 4-71. *Jump To (If bot recognises) with True condition for node to node on the same level*

If the condition does not evaluate to true, the system moves to the target node; it does not execute the response statement of the target node. It does not evaluate any conditions in the child nodes. It moves to the next sibling node to continue the evaluation of conditions in a top-down fashion.

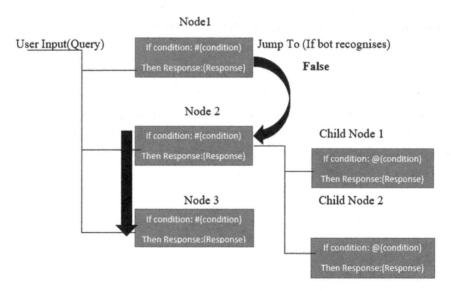

Figure 4-72. *Jump To (If bot recognises) with True condition for node to node on the same level*

Respond executes the response defined on the target node, irrespective of the condition being met or not met.

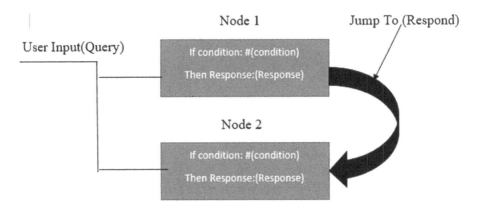

Figure 4-73. Jump To (Respond) for node to node on the same level

Conclusion

This chapter was a deep dive into the Watson Assistant service provided by IBM Cloud. It covered how we use the service to build a virtual cognitive bot from scratch.

We began with setting up an account and tried out the bot with the built-in assistant. You learned basic concepts, like intents, entities, and dialogs for configuring a use case. We went through all the features provided by the Watson dialog to make a bot provide a seamless conversation with a user.

CHAPTER 5

Advanced Concepts of Watson Agent

You have learned how to create a simple but useful chatbot. This chapter covers advanced topics, such as contextual entities, context variables, slots, and digressions, and how to handle multiple intents. These advanced features of the IBM Watson platform help solve complex use cases and create advanced workflows.

Contextual Entities

In the previous chapter, we used the @Policies entity to train the IBM Watson engine to determine if the policy mentioned in the conversation was health insurance or motor insurance.

There is another way in which entities can be marked directly: when entering variations for intent. A part of the variation can be marked as an entity value, which is known as an *annotation*.

The part of the intent that is marked as entity value is called a *mention*. The entities marked in this manner are called *contextual entities*.

© Navin Sabharwal, Sudipta Barua, Neha Anand, Pallavi Aggarwal 2020
N. Sabharwal et al., *Developing Cognitive Bots Using the IBM Watson Engine*,
https://doi.org/10.1007/978-1-4842-5555-1_5

You can better understand this with an example. Let's use a "Reset Password" use case for Outlook or Gmail. Let's define various elements for it.

- **Intent**: #Reset_Password

- **Entity**: Mailbox

- **Entity Values**: Outlook, Gmail

- **Variations**: Reset Password

  - Help me reset my password.

  - I want to reset my password in Outlook.

  - I want to reset my password in Gmail.

  - Reset my Gmail password.

  - Reset my Outlook password.

In the preceding intents, Gmail and Outlook are the entity values that we can mark as contextual entities. They are automatically added to the entity and show up in the entities' annotations section. The Annotation tab shows the intent for which these entities are marked.

Figure 5-1 shows the variations added to the intent.

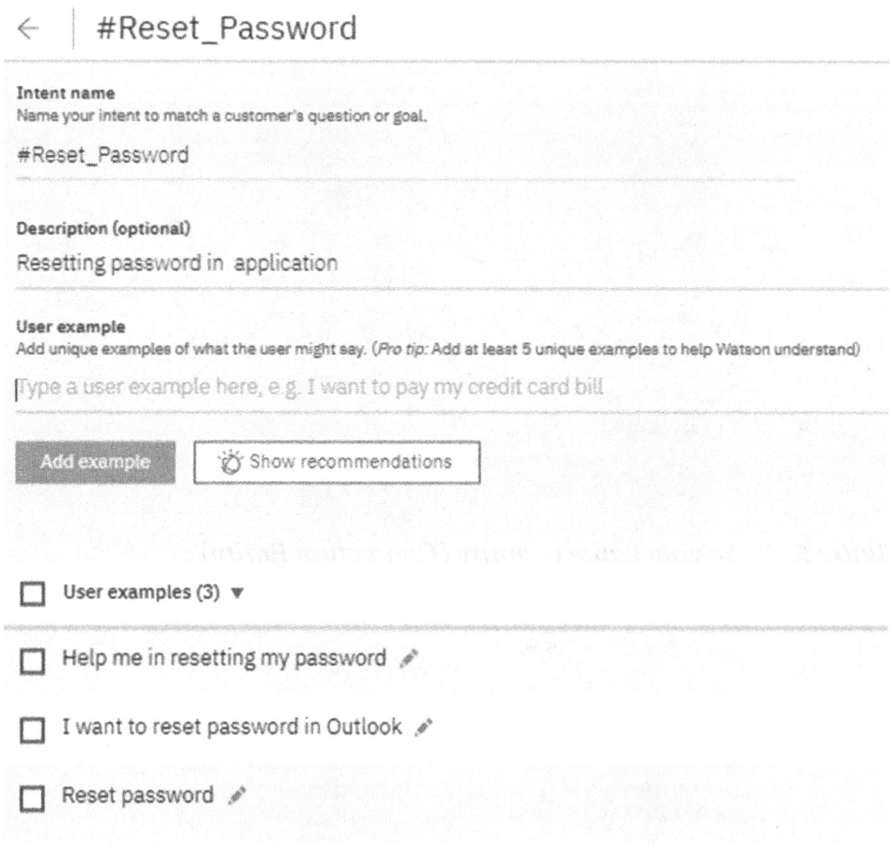

← | #Reset_Password

Intent name
Name your intent to match a customer's question or goal.

#Reset_Password

Description (optional)
Resetting password in application

User example
Add unique examples of what the user might say. (*Pro tip:* Add at least 5 unique examples to help Watson understand)

Type a user example here, e.g. I want to pay my credit card bill

[Add example]   [☼ Show recommendations]

☐ User examples (3) ▼

☐ Help me in resetting my password ✎

☐ I want to reset password in Outlook ✎

☐ Reset password ✎

Figure 5-1. *Variations added*

Let's proceed to mark entities from these intents.

We'll select the part or the term that we want to add as an entity value. Once selected, a pop-up window appears, as shown in Figure 5-2. If the entity is not defined, you can add the entity in the **Enter an entity name** field.

This adds the entity and the part of text that we marked earlier, which was Outlook, as shown in Figure 5-3.

Let's call the entity @Mailbox, and Outlook is added to this entity.

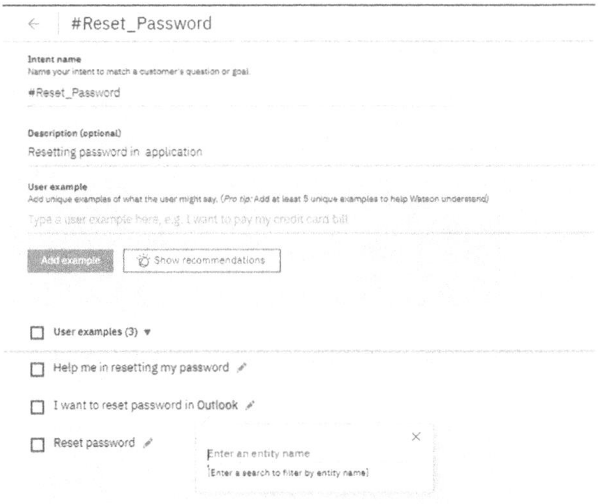

Figure 5-2. *Adding value to entity (Contextual Entity)*

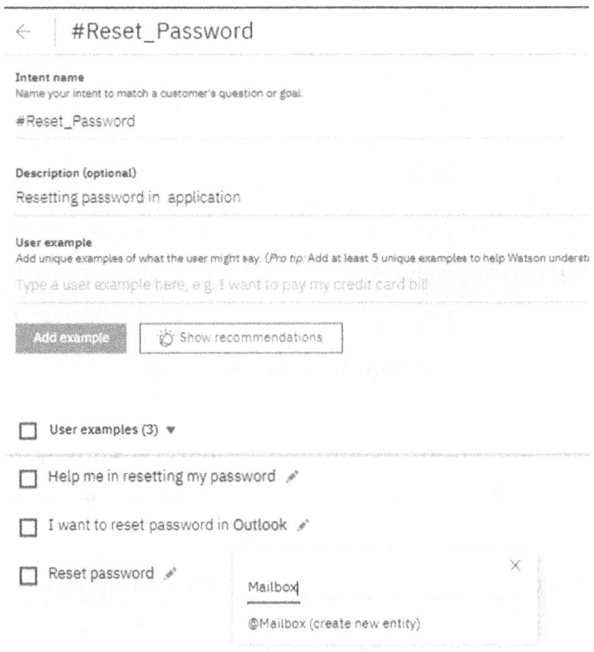

Figure 5-3. *Value added to entity (Contextual Entity)*

Go back to the Skill page and click the entity. The entity created @Mailbox with the Outlook value, as shown in Figures 5-4 and 5-5.

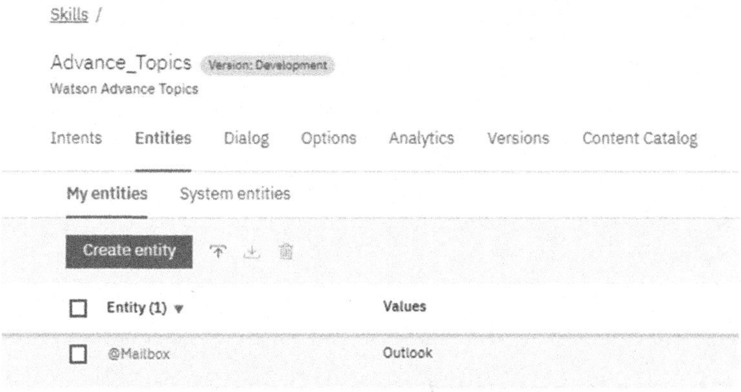

Skills /

Advance_Topics Version: Development
Watson Advance Topics

Intents   **Entities**   Dialog   Options   Analytics   Versions   Content Catalog

My entities   System entities

Create entity   ☁ ⬇ 🗑

☐   Entity (1) ▼   Values

☐   @Mailbox   Outlook

Figure 5-4. *Entity reflected on the Entity page*

Click the **@Mailbox** entity and then click the **Annotations** tab. You see the annotation and the entity that you marked while entering the variations, as shown in Figure 5-6.

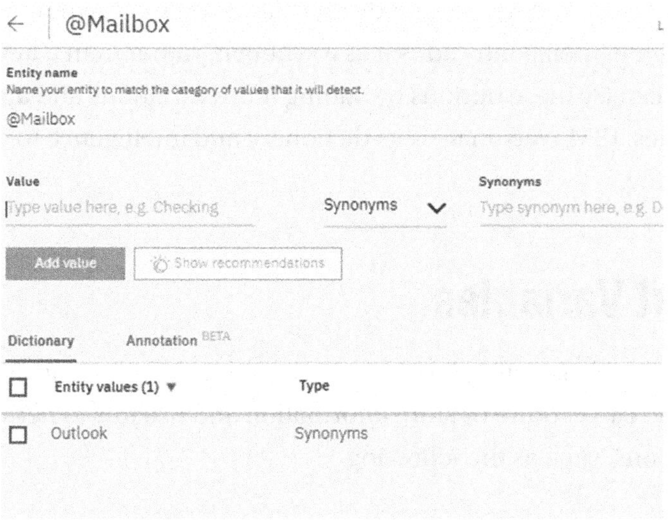

← | @Mailbox   L

Entity name
Name your entity to match the category of values that it will detect.

@Mailbox

Value   Synonyms
Type value here, e.g. Checking   Synonyms ∨   Type synonym here, e.g. D

Add value   ☼ Show recommendations

Dictionary   Annotation BETA

☐   Entity values (1) ▼   Type

☐   Outlook   Synonyms

Figure 5-5. *Value added to entity (Contextual Entity)*

107

← | @Mailbox

Entity name
Name your entity to match the category of values that it will detect.

@Mailbox

Dictionary   Annotation BETA

☐   User examples (1)   Intent ▼

☐   I want to reset password in **Outlook**   #Reset_Password

Figure 5-6. *Annotation added*

If we select another variation and try to mark an entity to add as a value, the previously marked entity (i.e., @Mailbox) shows up as an option that you can select.

If the entity value is for a new type of entity, then you can keep adding them from the same drop-down menu.

If there is an entity value already there, and you mark synonyms, the Watson engine intelligently adds it as a synonym rather than a new entity value. You can try these options by adding more variations and annotating these entities. IBM Watson uses its dictionary and intelligence to do this automatically.

Context Variables

A context variable is defined within a node with a default value. It is useful because you can capture or store information and use this to perform further actions, such as the following.

- **Passing context from the application:** The
  information is passed from the API/application to the
  dialog by setting a context variable and passing the
  context variable to the dialog.

- **Passing context from node to node:** You can pass
  the values of the context variables from one node to
  another node. This is helpful in resetting the context.

It is used in slots to define or store the value in the condition set.

You can enable it in the hamburger menu on a node's response field.
Select **Open context editor**, as shown in Figure 5-7, and save the required
context.

Figure 5-7. Open context editor

The context variables are shown with **$** (see Figure 5-8).

Then set context   ⋮

VARIABLE	VALUE
$ Enter variable	Enter value 🗑

Add variable ⊕

Figure 5-8. *Context variable editor*

Let's look at how context variables work for a node with "Reset Password" as a use case.

- **Intent**: #Reset_Password

- @Mailbox with Outlook and Gmail as their values

Let's configure the use case in the dialog, capture the values, and pass them on to the context variables. You will see how to use this context variable later in the workflow step.

On the Dialog page, add a node and name it. Set up the condition in the intent field and configure the dialog flow, as shown in Figure 5-9.

Figure 5-9. *Dialog node*

110

Navigate to the child nodes and enable the context variable by clicking the hamburger menu on the node page. Select **Open context editor**, as shown in Figure 5-10.

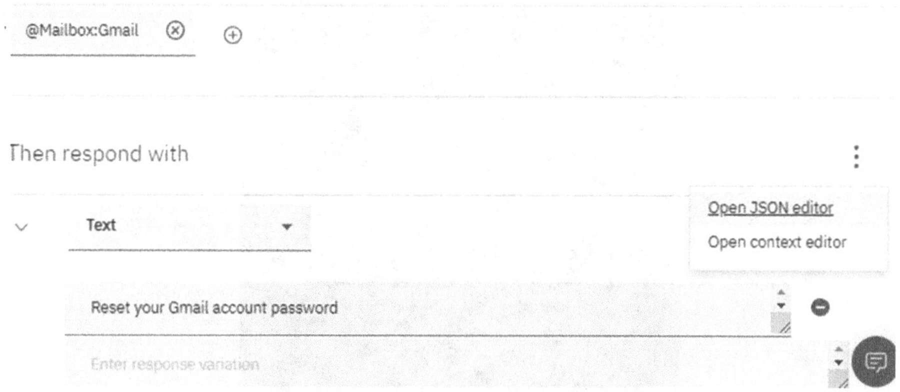

Figure 5-10. *Open context editor*

You can see the "**Then set context**" page. Add the variable as $Account that will capture the value of the account name as "Gmail" and will be used to reset the password, as shown in Figure 5-11. You can also do this for the Outlook account.

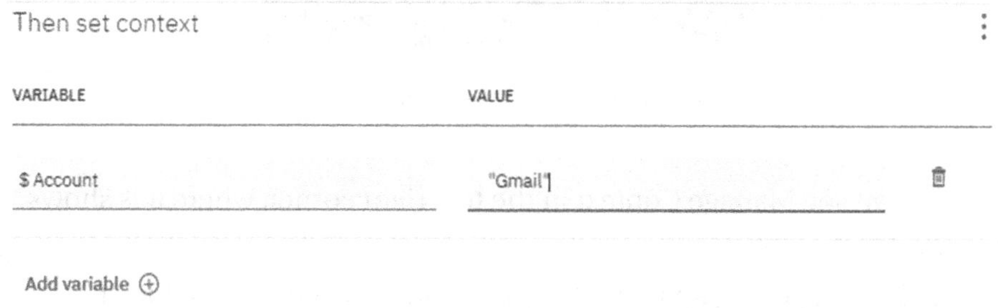

Figure 5-11. *Context variable defined*

When the user selects either of the options, then the value of the **$Account** context variable is set. If the user selects Gmail, then $Account is set to Gmail. If Outlook selected, then it is set to Outlook. You can check

111

whether the value of the context variable is set or not by clicking the Try It Out panel on the Dialog page. Click **Manage Context** to see the context variable value, as shown in Figure 5-12.

Figure 5-12. *User selected the account option*

You can see Manage Context in the top-right corner, where it is shows the number 2.

Click **Manage Context**. You see the $Account context variable and the value is set to Gmail since we selected the Gmail option. This is shown in Figure 5-13.

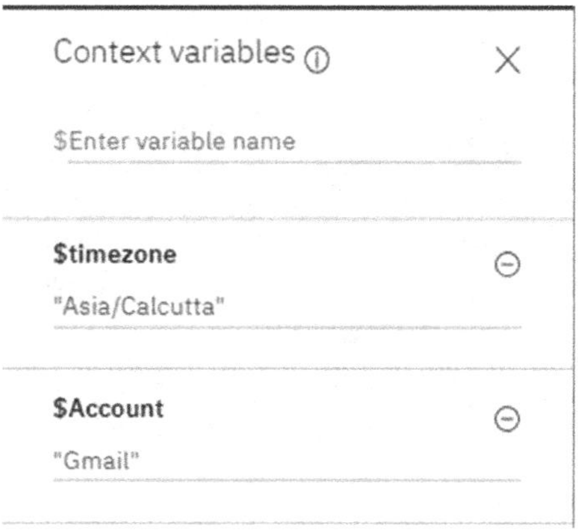

Context variables ⓘ   ✕

$Enter variable name

$timezone   ⊖
"Asia/Calcutta"

$Account   ⊖
"Gmail"

Figure 5-13. *Showing the context variable value*

Slots

The slots feature helps a dialog node gather or check multiple conditions within the same node itself.

The information that a user provides up front is saved, and the assistant asks only for the missing details that it needs to fulfill the request. It checks all the conditions defined in the slots and asks a prompting question. It proceeds only when all the conditions have been evaluated and met.

Let's try to better understand this in the following diagram. When the intent for the query is matched, it enters the node and asks the respective questions defined in slots 1 and 2 as shown in Figure 5-14. Once all the slots' conditions are met, it performs the next action. But if the conditions in either slot are not fulfilled, it keeps asking a prompting question.

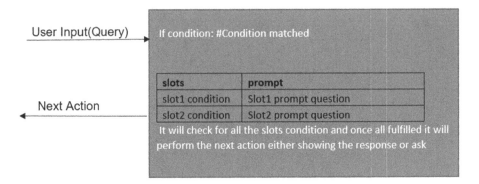

Figure 5-14. *Slot Feature*

You can enable it with the Customize button on the node, as shown in Figure 5-15.

Figure 5-15. *Customize button*

Click **Customize node** and select **Slots**. Move the slider to the **On** position and tick **Prompt for everything**. Click **Apply**, as shown in Figure 5-16.

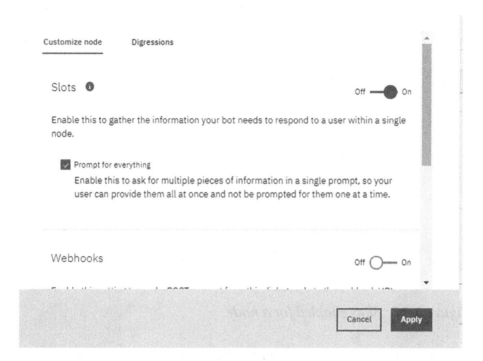

Figure 5-16. *Enabling the slots for a node*

After the slots are enabled for the node, the node appears, as shown in Figure 5-17.

Figure 5-17. *Slots enabled for a node*

After the slots are enabled, you see the **Then Check for** option. You can define the conditions as follows.

- CHECK FOR: Defines the conditions.

- SAVE IT AS: Saves the value in context variables.

- IF NOT PRESENT ASK: If the condition is not matched, then you can ask the prompting question.

Finally, enter a response in the Response field.

Let's better understand this by using the "Reset Password" example. We will define the slots in the node that check the condition (i.e., whether the account the user wants to reset password for is defined or not).

Enable the slots in the node by clicking the **Customize** button and then selecting **Slots**. Tick **Prompt for everything**. The steps to enable slots were covered earlier. After the slots are enabled, the node looks like what is shown in Figure 5-18.

Reset Password   Customize ✿   ✕
_____

If assistant recognizes:

#Reset_Password   ⊗   ⊕
_____

Then check for: ⓘ Manage handlers

CHECK FOR	SAVE IT AS	IF NOT PRESENT, ASK	TYPE
1 Enter condition	Enter variable	Enter prompt	Optional ✿ 🗑

Figure 5-18. *Slots enabled for the node*

1. Delete the child nodes. You are going to handle
   the condition check for the account and set up the
   context variable in the same node.

2. In CHECK FOR, define the condition for the account
   to be checked. Set it to a context variable, as shown
   in Figure 5-19.

Reset Password   Customize ⚙   ✕

If assistant recognizes:

#Reset_Password   ⊗   ⊕

Then check for: ⓿ Manage handlers

	CHECK FOR	SAVE IT AS	IF NOT PRESENT, ASK	TYPE		
1	@Mailbox	$Account	Currently I am traine	Required	⚙	🗑

Figure 5-19. *Slot condition filled for checking the account*

3. We have defined the condition in CHECK FOR as
    @Mailbox, so it will check whether the user has
    entered the account (Gmail or Outlook) for which
    he wants to reset the password.

4. If the condition is matched, the user has defined the
    account. The value of the $Account context variable is
    set to Gmail or Outlook. If not, then it asks the IF NOT
    PRESENT, ASK question, as shown in Figure 5-20.

Figure 5-20. *Slots condition not fulfilled and prompt question shown*

5. In the right corner, you find the gear button ⚙
    where you have defined the slots. Clicking it takes
    you to the page shown in Figure 5-21, where you can
    set the response.

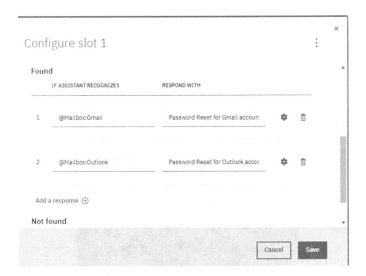

Figure 5-21. *Slot Found, Not found condition set*

In this section, you learned how to configure slots for different scenarios in a node. You also learned how to set the context variables within slots.

Multiple Responses (Multiple Conditioned Responses)

With this feature, we can provide different responses to the same input, based on the other conditions provided. A single node can provide several different responses; each of the responses is triggered by a different condition. This approach helps simplify the dialog tree structure.

1. Navigate to a node in the dialog, and click the Customize button to enable it, as shown in Figure 5-22.

Figure 5-22. *Customize button on a node*

2. Click the Customize node and scroll down to the
    Multiple conditioned responses option. Click the
    slider On and click **Apply**, as shown in Figure 5-23.

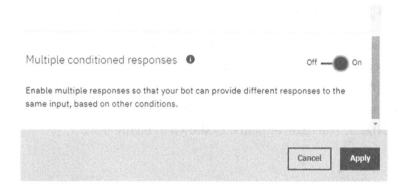

Figure 5-23. *Enabling Multiple conditioned responses*

After applying **Multiple conditioned response** on the node, the node
appears, as shown in Figure 5-24.

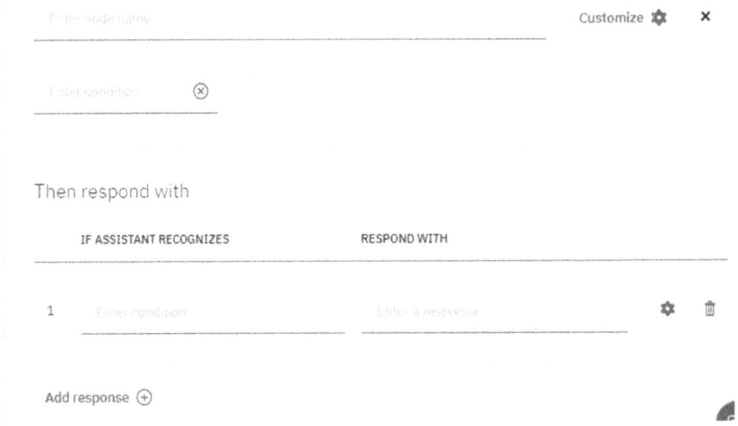

Figure 5-24. *Node with Multiple conditioned responses enabled*

Let's see how this works by taking the "Reset Password" use case. Delete the child nodes and navigate to the node where we have simply defined the intent condition. This enables the **Multiple conditioned response** option and sets the condition in IF ASSISTANT RECOGNIZES. The node appears, as shown in Figure 5-25.

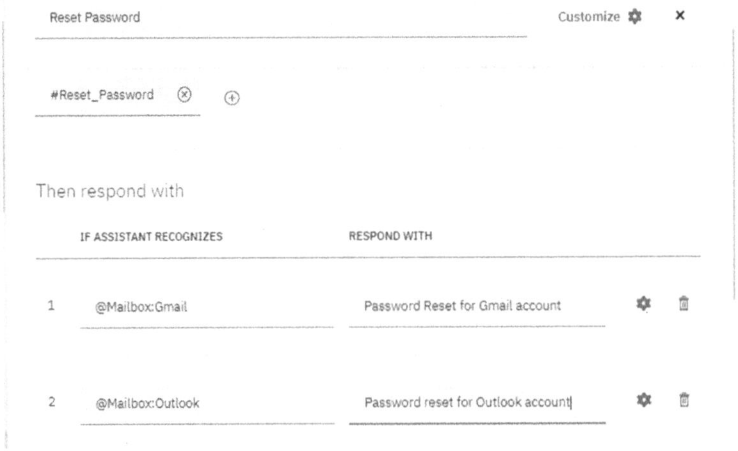

Figure 5-25. *Multiple conditioned responses with different conditions within the same node*

122

This way, we reduce the tree structure and check the condition in the same node, showing the respective responses. The same use case can be configured in slots using context variables with multiple conditioned responses. We can avoid this step and do this from within one node.

The basic differences between slots and multiple conditioned responses is that slots force you to go through all the options and provide the option to set context variables. You can choose the right option for your use case based on this.

Digression

Digression is a way to achieve context switching. You can handle the scenario where user starts one use case and moves through the dialog but suddenly asks a different query that is related to a different use case.

In this scenario, we need to complete the digressed workflow and then come back to the original use case that the user initiated.

Let's discuss digression with the "Reset Password" and the "Configure Out of Office" use cases. The example will digress between the dialogs and resume the original workflow after completing the digressed workflow.

Download Advance_Topics-Slots_Digression.json for the "Configure Out of Office" and "Reset Password" use cases from `https://github.com/watson05/Cognitive-Bot`. Refer to Chapter 4 for how to import a JSON file into a Watson agent.

The two use cases are configured in the dialog in Figure 5-26.

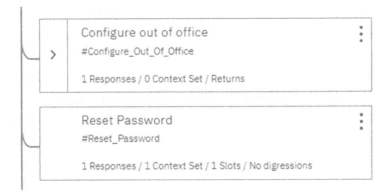

Figure 5-26. *Two use cases shown for digression*

The user enters the query as "I want to reset password." Watson Assistant provides options to select either Gmail or Outlook. Rather than selecting an option, the user enters, "I want to configure out of office." Since the user has asked something entirely different from the current use case, the workflow digresses to the node where the "Configure Out of Office" use case is configured, and then performs the steps.

To achieve this, navigate to the node from where you want to digress. Enable the digressions for that node. Click **Customize** and then select **Digressions**. The node has a pop-up for selecting and enabling the options, as shown in Figure 5-27.

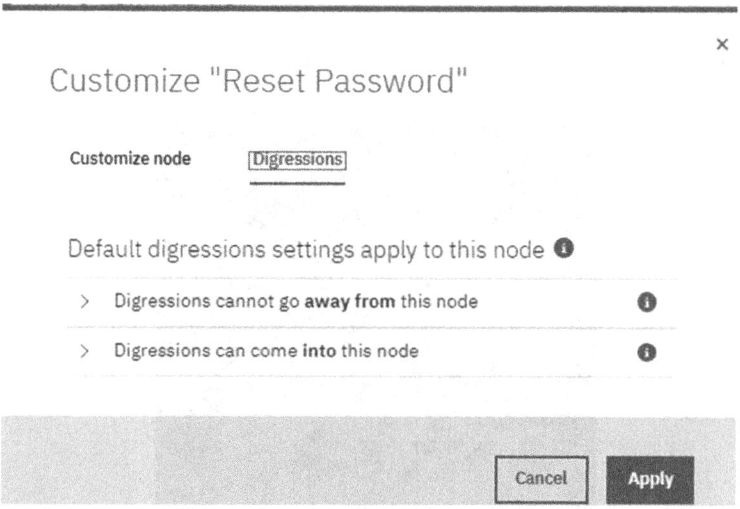

Figure 5-27. *Digression selected*

Select the first option and switch it On. Click **Apply**, as shown in Figure 5-28.

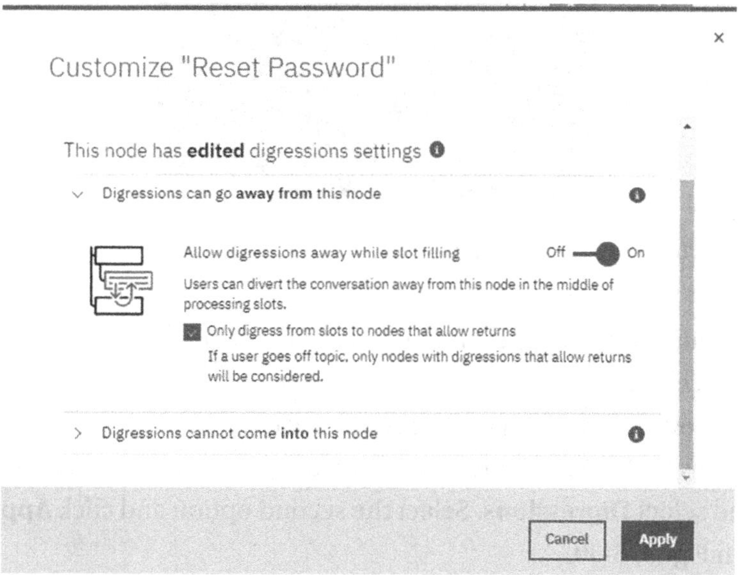

Figure 5-28. *Select option 1 from Digression*

Let's see if the dialog handles the change by navigating to the Dialog page and clicking **Try it out**, as shown in Figure 5-29.

Figure 5-29. *Try it out result*

The dialog found the new intent but did not digress to the "Configure Out of Office" workflow.

To achieve a digression to the correct use case, you have to make a few changes to the "Configure Out of Office" use case dialog. Click the node and select **Digressions**. Select the second option and click **Apply**, as shown in Figure 5-30.

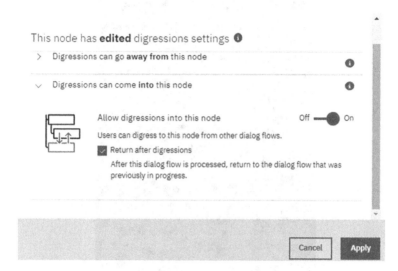

Figure 5-30. *Select option 2 from Digression*

We are simply configuring this node to allow for digressions to come into this node from elsewhere in the workflow. Having done this, use the Try It Out panel to see the results, as shown in Figures 5-31 and 5-32.

Figure 5-31. *Trying out the use case*

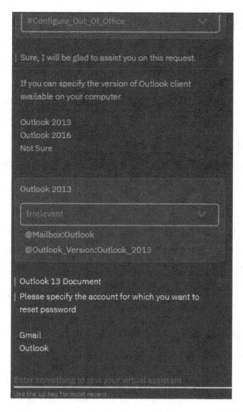

Figure 5-32. *Digression done*

You can see that the conversation took the following route.

1.   The user selects the "Reset Password" use case.

2.   The intent changes to the "Configure Out of Office" use case.

3.   The dialog moves the user to the correct workflow and completes the workflow "Configure Out of Office" workflow.

4.   The dialog moves back to the original "Reset Password" workflow.

5.   The user completes the "Reset Password" scenario.

Disambiguation

Disambiguation is the ability of the system to take ambiguous data and make sense out of it.

Ambiguity in terms of Watson conversations is encountered when the utterances from a user can mean one of many things and two or more use cases configured in Watson are in conflict.

We'll use an example to better understand the disambiguation feature.

Let's use the "Reset Password" use case for this scenario. The user simply asks "reset my password" without specifying either Gmail or Outlook. Since the user has provided ambiguous or incomplete information, the system should probe to disambiguate the scenario. Let's get this configured to see how it works.

You can download the skill JSON that has the use case configured for disambiguation.

Go to GitHub (`https://github.com/watson05/Cognitive-Bot`) to download Advance_Topics-Disambiguation.json.

The intents and variations are as follows and shown in Figure 5-33. Note that this use case is configured differently than the one in earlier examples.

- **Intent**: #Reset_Password_Gmail
    - Help me reset my Gmail password.
    - How can I reset my Gmail password?
    - I want to reset my password in Gmail.
- **Intent:** #Reset_Password_Outlook
    - Help me reset my Outlook password.
    - How can I reset my Outlook password?
    - I want to reset my password in Outlook.

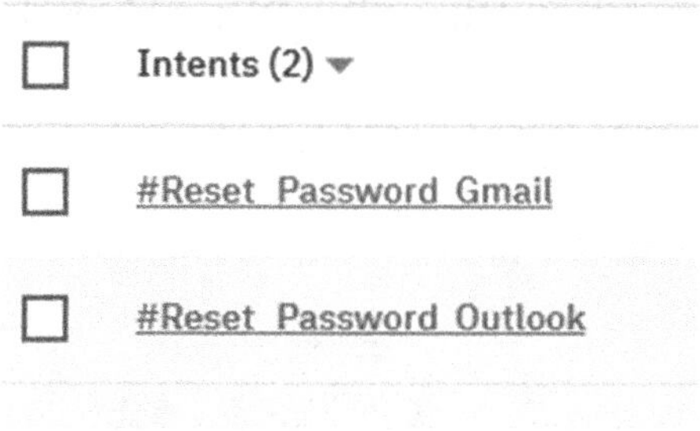

☐ Intents (2) ▼

☐ #Reset_Password_Gmail

☐ #Reset_Password_Outlook

Figure 5-33. *Intents added*

Go to the Dialog page and add two nodes. Configure the two use cases with the defined conditions and the responses, as shown in Figure 5-34.

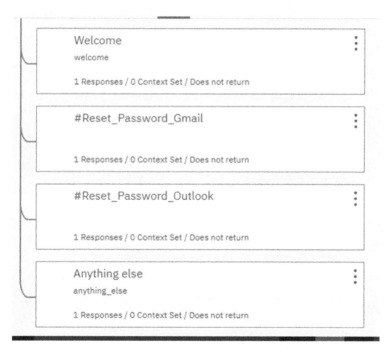

Figure 5-34. *Dialog page with use cases configured*

Select the **Options** tab and then click **Disambiguation**, as shown in Figure 5-35.

Intents   Entities   Dialog   **Options**   Analytics   Versions   Content Catalog

Webhooks

Disambiguation

Autocorrection

System Entities

Disambiguation

If your skill is confident that more than one dialog node can address a user's query, disambiguation allows the assistant to ask the user for clarification. A description of the purpose of each dialog node is displayed as a list of options, and the user is asked to pick the right one. Learn more

Off ◯── On

Figure 5-35. *Options page with Disambiguation selected*

Turn the slider **On** and enter the information, as shown in Figure 5-36.

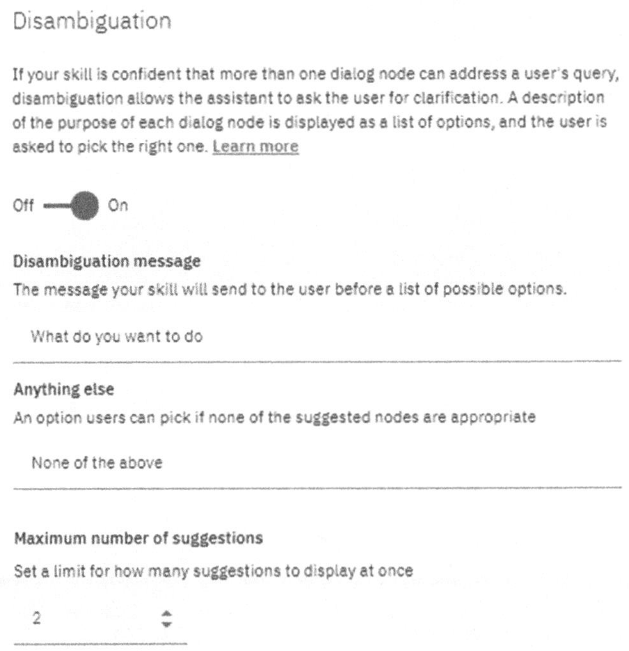

Disambiguation

If your skill is confident that more than one dialog node can address a user's query, disambiguation allows the assistant to ask the user for clarification. A description of the purpose of each dialog node is displayed as a list of options, and the user is asked to pick the right one. Learn more

Off ──● On

Disambiguation message
The message your skill will send to the user before a list of possible options.

What do you want to do

Anything else
An option users can pick if none of the suggested nodes are appropriate

None of the above

Maximum number of suggestions
Set a limit for how many suggestions to display at once

2   ⬍

Figure 5-36. *Disambiguation page*

Go back to the Dialog page and click the use case nodes. The **If virtual-assistant needs to represent node to users, then use** field is shown in Figure 5-37. This feature or the field's status is locked (in red) because no response has been added.

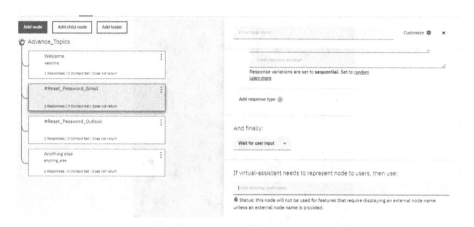

Figure 5-37. *If virtual-assistant needs to represent node to users, then use field*

Add the response option for user to select when the user's query has a conflict between two similar use cases, as shown in Figure 5-38.

Figure 5-38. *If virtual-assistant needs to represent node to users, then use field*

Once the response is added, then the status becomes unlocked (in green).

Repeat this for the "Reset Password in Outlook" use case.

After configuring for both the nodes, try the use case in Watson's Try It Out panel to see the results, as shown in Figure 5-39.

Figure 5-39. *Options shown*

Select either option and the use case is executed, as shown in Figure 5-40.

Figure 5-40. *Options result shown*

Disambiguation provides an easy way to handle conflicts in intents or incomplete information provided by the user. So, it triggers the relevant use case based on the confidence score returned when the query is entered. The confidence score is a threshold value by Watson that helps to recognize the top intents matched from the array of intents returned.

Handling Multiple Intents

There are scenarios when user asks a query that has more than one intent; for example, "Reset password and unlock account." The bot can only perform or execute one action at a time. The bot must understand that the user is asking a question that has two different intents and then execute the two use cases in a step-by-step fashion.

To achieve this, there is a node that disambiguates the different intents. Let's use the Watson feature called *the confidence score* to solve this use case. The confidence score is a score assigned to the array of intents when a query is entered into the system.

We will use the confidence score in a node that checks the confidence score of the top intents returned for the query entered. They are defined as follows.

- Intents[0].confidence is the confidence of the highest matching intent

- Intents[1].confidence is the confidence of the second highest matching intent

Intents[1].confidence checks if the confidence score of the second-highest matching intent is greater than 20 percent. Intents[0].confidence checks if the highest matching intent is more than 95 percent. The values set to check the confidence score can be changed as per the use case.

If these conditions are matched, then the bot responds with a message saying, "Which of these options do you want to perform?" It presents the two options that map to the two intents.

Let's see how to get this configured in the dialog. The use cases are configured and shown in Figure 5-41.

- Reset Password in Outlook

- Reset Password in Gmail

- Unlock Password

Figure 5-41. *Use cases Nodes added*

The Welcome node that provides the greeting message waits for user input. Add a $disambiguated context variable and set its value to null, as shown in Figure 5-42.

Figure 5-42. *Disambiguate context variable added in Welcome node*

Now let's add a node that disambiguates between the intents. Add a node above the configured use cases and enter the confidence condition as **(intents[1].confidence>0.2 && intents[0].confidence<0.95)**. This checks the confidence score of the intents returned. An intents array stores the confidence score of intents in decreasing order. Thus, intents[0] has the highest confidence score followed by intents[1], as shown in Figure 5-43.

Figure 5-43. *Confidence score condition defined*

To display the intents captured as options for user to select, we can set these values in the context variable and further reuse them as options, as shown in Figure 5-44.

```
"intent0label": "<? intents[0].intent.replace('_',' ') ?>",
"intent0score": "<? T(String).format('%.0f',intents[0].
confidence*100) ?>",
"intent1label": "<? intents[1].intent.replace('_',' ') ?>",
"intent1score": "<? T(String).format('%.0f',intents[0].
confidence*100) ?>",
"disambiguated": true
```

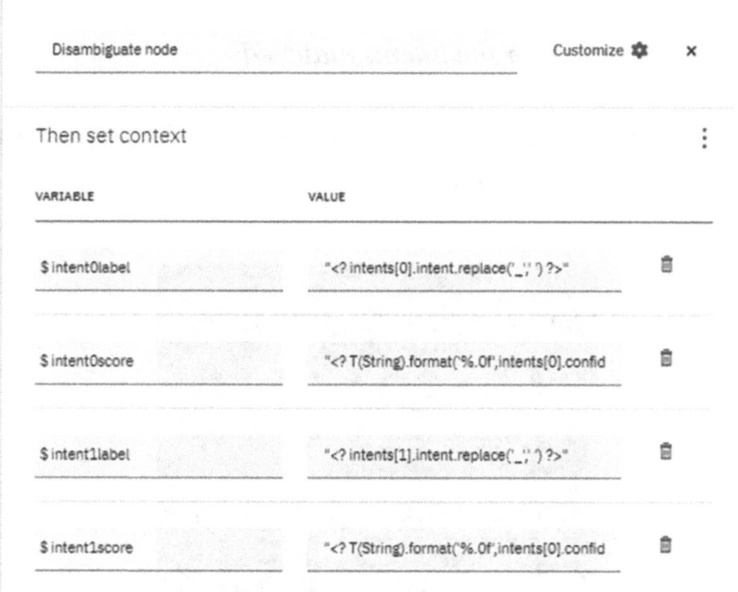

Figure 5-44. *Context variables defined to capture the top intents matched*

Next, we need to show these options. We can do this in the **And respond with** field, as shown in Figure 5-45.

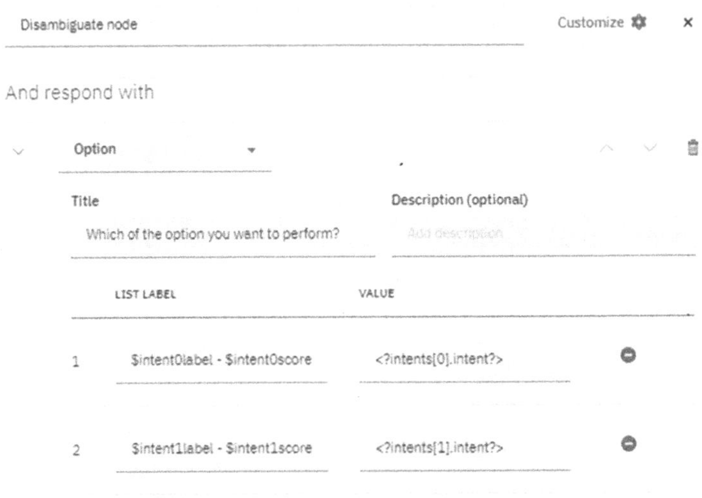

| Disambiguate node | | | Customize ⚙ | ✕ |

And respond with

| ⌄ | Option ▾ | | ⌃ ⌄ | 🗑 |

Title

Which of the option you want to perform?

Description (optional)

Add description

	LIST LABEL	VALUE	
1	$intent0label - $intent0score	<?intents[0].intent?>	⊖
2	$intent1label - $intent1score	<?intents[1].intent?>	⊖

Figure 5-45. *Options for the intents matched*

Let's try the use case in the Watson Try It Out panel to see the results, as shown in Figure 5-46 and Figure 5-47.

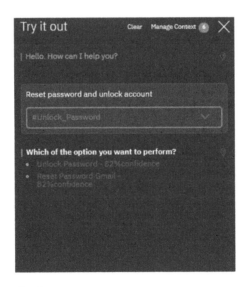

Figure 5-46. *Result shown*

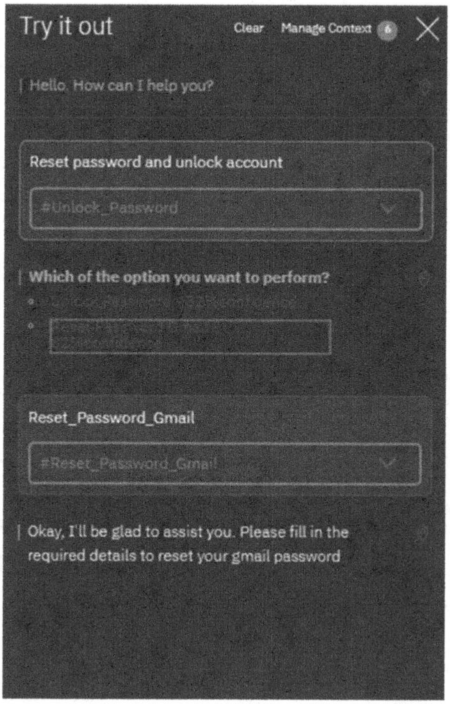

Figure 5-47. *Result shown*

You can see that the two intents were identified based on the confidence score, so the bot responded with a prompting response with the intents as options.

Showcasing Solutions in Various Formats

Text

You can provide the bot's response in text format by selecting **Text** from the responses drop-down in the node field, as shown in Figure 5-48.

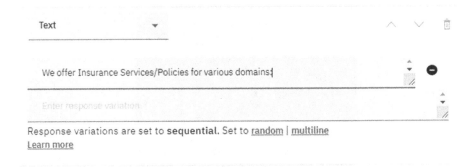

Figure 5-48. *Response*

HTML

If you want to show content in a rich format in HTML, like a table or form, you can do it in the response section. Simply paste the HTML content in the response section, as shown in Figure 5-49.

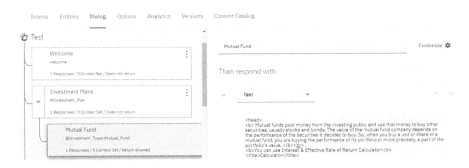

Figure 5-49. *Response added*

Options

If you want to showcase options as buttons, then select Options from the drop-down menu, as shown in Figures 5-50 and 5-51.

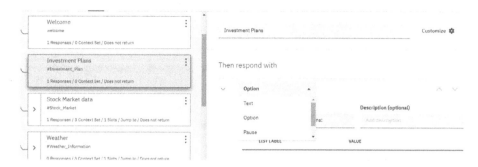

Figure 5-50. *Drop-down in Then Respond with*

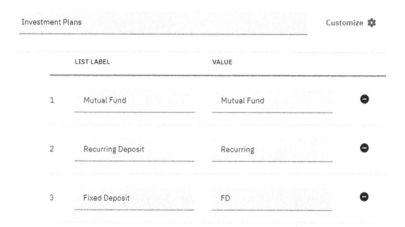

Figure 5-51. *Option value added*

Conclusion

This chapter concludes with various advanced features to enhance a bot's conversational capabilities. We explained topics such as context variables, slots, multiple response, digressions, and disambiguation with examples that reduced the conflicts and node structures by handling multiple things in the same node.

CHAPTER 6

Use Cases for Cognitive Virtual Bots

In this chapter, we describe use case configurations for various domains and learn how to use IBM Cloud to accomplish a particular goal, such as integrating the Watson Assistant with external APIs. IBM Cloud Functions is a serverless execution environment for building and connecting cloud services. A cloud function lets you focus on writing code and building solutions without building or maintaining a complex infrastructure.

Domain-Specific Use Cases for BFSI

In the BFSI domain, we will take up an end customer use case where a consumer can inquire about various investment options.

We will name our use case "Investment Plans" and move on to the next step, which is identifying the intents, entities, and variations.

- **Intent Description:** Find the types of investment plans available from a provider.

- **Intent Name: #Investment_Plan**

- **Entity:** Investment Plans Types

- **Entity Values:** Mutual Fund, Recurring Deposit, Fixed Deposit, Systematic Investment Plan.

© Navin Sabharwal, Sudipta Barua, Neha Anand, Pallavi Aggarwal 2020
N. Sabharwal et al., *Developing Cognitive Bots Using the IBM Watson Engine*,
https://doi.org/10.1007/978-1-4842-5555-1_6

With this basic data populated, we need utterances or variations from the end users; that is, how they will ask for this information. The following are a few examples of utterances. You can make the list richer by adding more utterances.

- I want to make an investment.

- Suggest some plans to make an investment.

- What are the different investment plans?

Let's now move to the IBM Watson console and configure the use case.

1. After logging in to IBM Cloud, launch the AI service created in an earlier chapter: "Watson Assistant – Virtual Bot".

2. Click **Skills** and then select the skill named Test.

3. In the top menu bar, choose **Intent**. The intent is named with a # sign followed by the name of the intent. We will call our intent #Investment_Plan.

4. Enter a brief description of the intent that you are creating. The **Add user example** option appears.

5. Enter the variations that we defined earlier, as shown in Figure 6-1. These are the sample variations that are fed into the Watson engine for training.

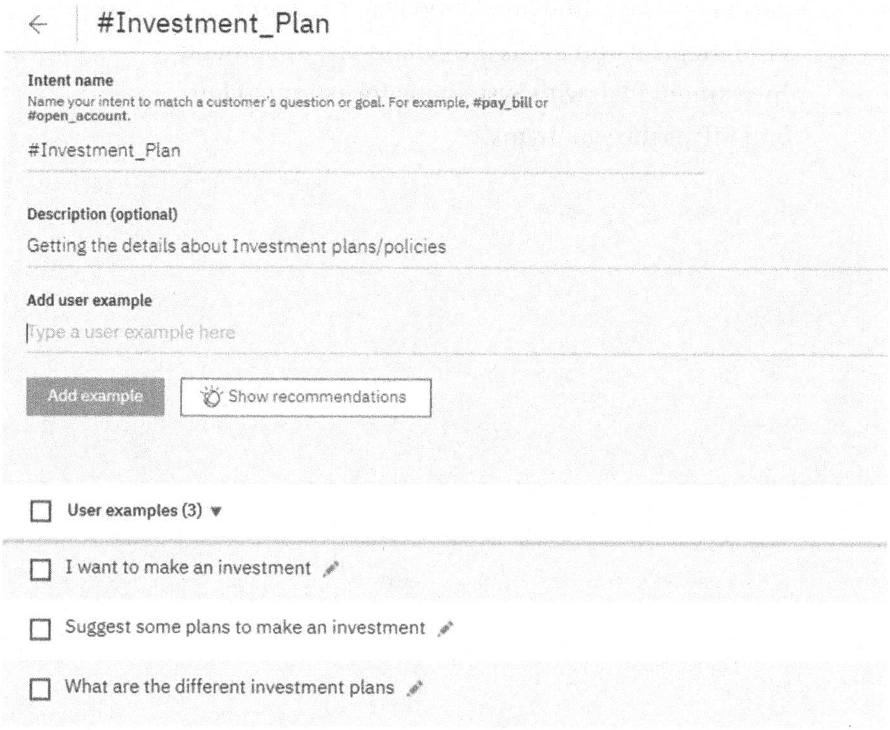

← | #Investment_Plan

Intent name

Name your intent to match a customer's question or goal. For example, #pay_bill or #open_account.

#Investment_Plan

Description (optional)

Getting the details about Investment plans/policies

Add user example

Type a user example here

| Add example | ☼ Show recommendations |

☐ **User examples (3)** ▼

☐ I want to make an investment ✐

☐ Suggest some plans to make an investment ✐

☐ What are the different investment plans ✐

Figure 6-1. *Intent page for adding the variations*

You are done configuring the intent and its variations, but we still haven't configured the entities for the system to decipher what the user wants.

1. To do this click, the **Back** button to go back to the Skill page.

2. Select **Entities** from the top menu. You are presented with a screen, as shown in Figure 6-2.

3. Enter *@Investment_Types* in Entity name. For the values, add Mutual Fund with Mutual Fund as the synonym; Recurring Deposit with Recurring Deposit

147

and RD as the synonyms; Fixed Deposit with
Fixed deposit and FD as the synonyms; Systematic
Investment Plan with Systematic Investment Plan
and SIP as the synonyms.

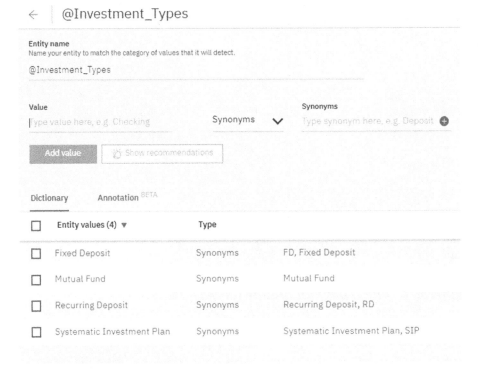

Figure 6-2. *Entity page*

After completing the configuration of the entities, intents, and
variations, we need to tie it all down using a dialog.

Let's add a node in the skill, as explained in the previous chapter.

1. Click the node and name it Investment Plans, as
    shown in Figure 6-3.

2. In the **Enter condition** field, provide the intent
    (i.e., *#Investment_Plan)*, as shown in Figure 6-3.

Figure 6-3. *Dialog node with intent defined in the condition*

3. In the Then respond with field, provide the response that you want to show when the condition is matched.

4. The Investment Plans use case four options: Mutual Fund, Recurring Deposit, Fixed Deposit, and Systematic Investment Plan. Click the node and select Option from the **Then respond with** drop-down menu. Add the options, as shown in Figure 6-4.

Investment Plans		Customize ⚙
⌄ Option ▼		∧ ⌄

Title	Description (optional)
We offer listed Investment Plans:	Add description

	LIST LABEL	VALUE	
1	Mutual Fund	Mutual Fund	⊖
2	Recurring Deposit	Recurring Deposit	⊖
3	Fixed Deposit	Fixed Deposit	⊖
4	Systematic Investment Plan	Systematic Investment Plan	⊖

Figure 6-4. *Dialog node defining Response field giving options*

149

Each option needs to be added as an entity with entity values, as you have already created in the Entity section. You have to manually ensure that the options match; there is no automatic check.

5. Return to the node and click the hamburger menu. Select **Add child node**. Since we have four options, add four child nodes.

6. Define the entity and entity value conditions in the child nodes (i.e., *@Investment_Types:(Mutual Fund), @Investment_Types:(Fixed Deposit), @Investment_Types:(Recurring Deposit), @Investment_Types:(Systematic Investment Plan),* as shown in Figure 6-5.

7. Add the response that you want to show in the response field of the respective child node when any option is selected, as shown in Figure 6-5.

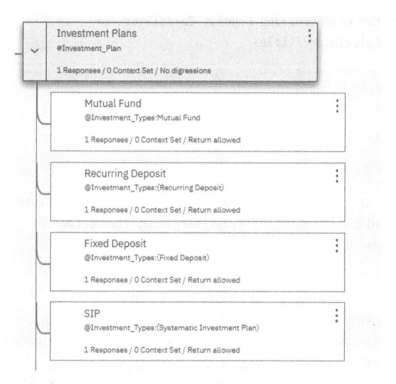

Figure 6-5. *Dialog node with Entity defined in the condition of child node*

We'll calculate the investment plan for each child node and show it through HTML code. The following sample HTML code is for the Recurring Deposit investment plan.

```
<html>
<head>
<b> A recurring deposit is a special kind of term deposit
offered by banks in India which help people with regular
incomes to deposit a fixed amount every month into their
recurring deposit account and earn interest at the rate
applicable to fixed deposits.</b><br>
```

```
<b>You can use Recurring Deposit Calculator</b>
<title>Calculator</title>
<style>
</style>
<script>

</script>
</head>
<body>
<iframe src=https://widgetscode.com/wc/rdm/all?skin=dblue0
style='width:280px;height:320px;margin:0;'frameborder=0>
</iframe>
</body>
</html>
```

Now we will use the functionality to show a calculator within the Watson Assistant. To do this, we add the code in the Recurring Deposit response field.

Add the HTML code in the **Then respond with** field of the child node, as shown in Figure 6-6.

Recurring Deposit   Customize ⚙   ✕

@Investment_Types:(Recurring Deposit)   ⊗   ⊕

Then respond with   ⋮

⌄   Text   ▾   ⌃ ⌄   🗑

```
<html>
<head>
<b> A recurring deposit is a special kind of term deposit offered by banks in India
which help people with regular incomes to deposit a fixed amount every month into
their recurring deposit account and earn interest at the rate applicable to fixed
deposits.</b><br>

<b>You can use Recurring Deposit Calculator</b>
<title>Calculator</title>
<style>
</style>
<script>

</script>
</head>
<body>
<iframe src=https://widgetscode.com/wc/rdm/all?skin=dblue0
style="width:280px;height:320px;margin:0;frameborder=0></iframe>
</body>
</html>
```

Figure 6-6. *Add HTML code in the Then respond with field*

Now let's try our use case on the bot that we created in the previous chapter, which is linked to the skill, as shown in Figure 6-7.

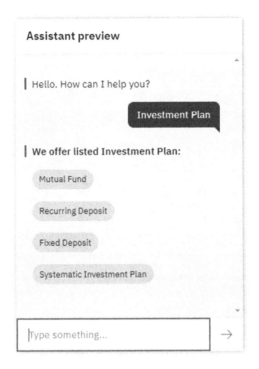

Figure 6-7. *Trying the use case and showing options to select*

Select the Recurring Deposit option. The result is shown in Figure 6-8.

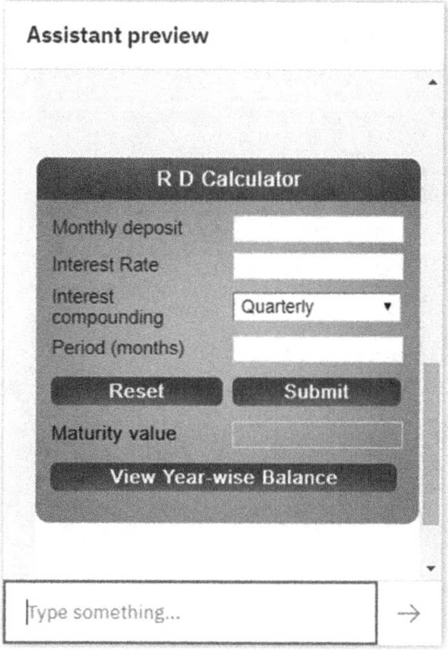

Figure 6-8. *Bot preview showing RD calculator*

Let's add the values in the field and calculate the RD. Click the **Submit** button to see the result. We can show complex use cases with calculations within the Watson Assistant GUI, as shown in Figure 6-9.

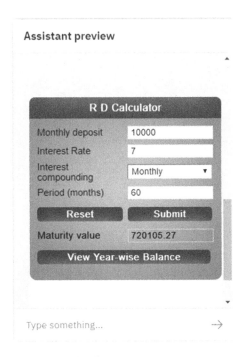

Figure 6-9. *Bot preview calculating RD*

Introduction to IBM Cloud Functions

IBM Cloud Functions are based on Apache Open Whisk, which is a Function as a Service (FaaS) platform that executes a function in response to incoming events. IBM Cloud Functions is a serverless execution environment for building and connecting cloud services. It is similar in functionality to other serverless options available from other cloud providers, like AWS Lambda, Google Cloud Functions, and Microsoft Azure Functions.

Let's look at a basic introduction to IBM Cloud Functions and then use them to integrate with third-party APIs to further enrich our bot.

IBM Cloud Functions makes it easy to integrate services by triggering actions from events.

To set up an IBM Cloud function, go to the IBM Cloud Catalog menu at `https://cloud.ibm.com/catalog`.

You are redirected to the Catalog page, as shown in Figure 6-10.

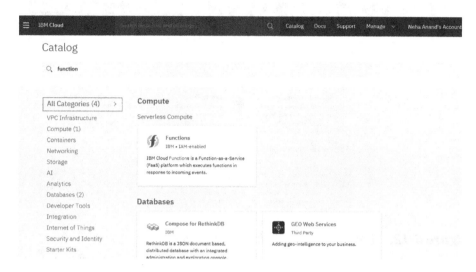

Figure 6-10. *IBM Cloud Catalog page*

Search for **function** and click the **Functions** service.

Click **Start Creating**, as shown in Figure 6-11.

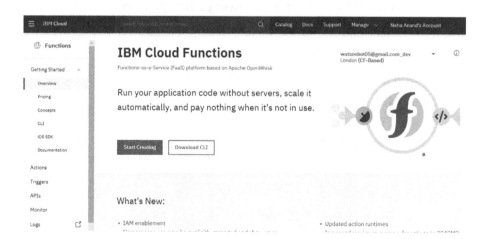

Figure 6-11. *IBM Cloud Functions page*

Click the **Create Action** tab, where the function code is invoked by REST API calls, as shown in Figure 6-12.

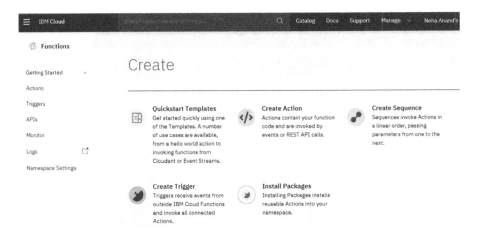

Figure 6-12. *IBM Cloud create function page*

Define the Cloud Functions action, as shown in Figure 6-13.

1. Type your action name [action_name] (e.g., Hello-World).

2. Create a package under **Enclosing Package** with any [package_name] (e.g., Assistant-Function).

3. Select the **Runtime** language. In this example, we will use Node.js.

4. Click the **Create** button.

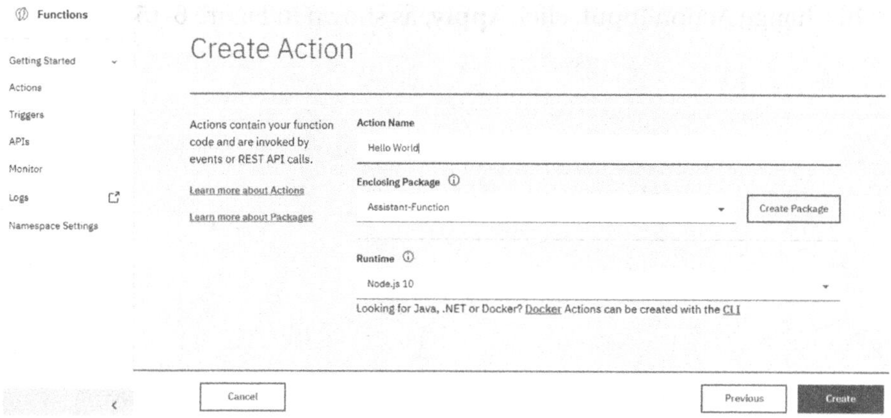

Figure 6-13. IBM cloud create Action page

We can now start editing the function. Let's write a simple "Hello World" example.

```
function main(params){
var greeting = 'Hello, ' + params.name;
return {greeting};
}
```

Run it in IBM Cloud Functions, as shown in Figure 6-14.

Figure 6-14. IBM Cloud function code console

In Change Action Input, click **Apply**, as shown in Figure 6-15.

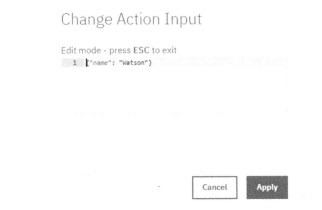

Figure 6-15. IBM Cloud function to add input parameter

Click the **Invoke** button to get the result, as shown in Figure 6-16.

Figure 6-16. IBM Cloud function with Activations results

Domain-Specific Use Cases for the Stock Market

This use case describes how to integrate the Watson Assistant with a stock API that is an external source (via an HTTP REST API service call). The user can enquire about a company's share price, and the bot responds with the current stock price, opening price, closing price, low price, and high price. We will use Cloud Functions to achieve this functionality.

Let's go through the steps to integrate Watson with an open source stock API.

Open Source Stock API

Go to `https://iexcloud.io/cloud-login#/register` to get an open source stock API. You are redirected to the page shown in Figure 6-17.

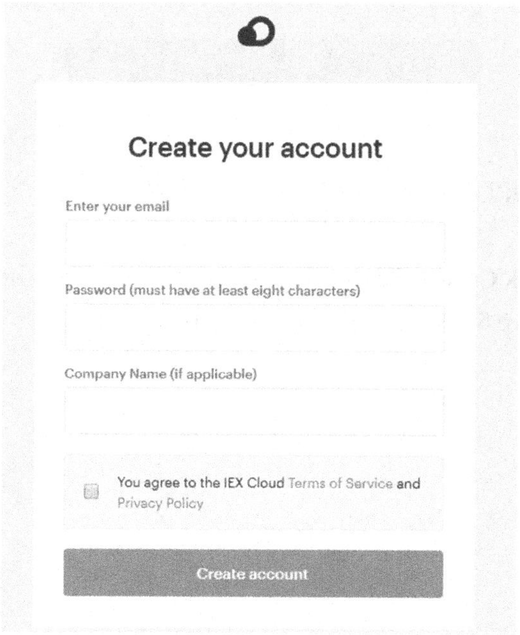

Figure 6-17. *Sign Up page*

161

Entered the required information to create an account, as shown in Figure 6-18.

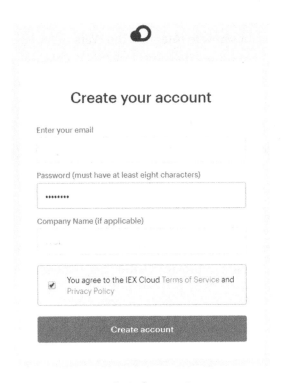

Figure 6-18. *Sign up page with information*

After you click **Create Account**, you are redirected to the Plan window, as shown in Figure 6-19. Click the **Select Start** option.

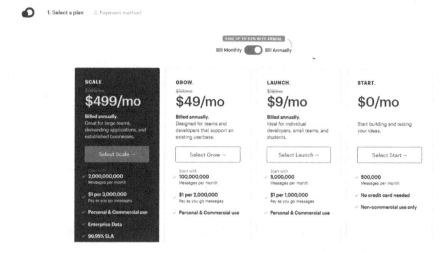

Figure 6-19. *Plan window*

To activate the account, you need to verify the email account. You see a verification message, as shown in Figure 6-20.

Figure 6-20. *Email verification page*

A confirmation email is sent to your registered email address. To access your API, go to the link mentioned in the confirmation mail, as shown in Figure 6-21.

IEX Cloud Email Verification

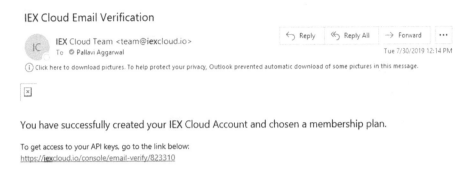

Figure 6-21. Confirmation mail screenshot

Go to the API Tokens tab and get your secret token key to access the API, as shown in Figure 6-22.

Figure 6-22. API Tokens page

The Base URL for the API is:

`https://cloud.iexapis.com/stable/stock/aapl/`
`quote?token=<YOUR_TOKEN_HERE>`

Replace <YOUR TOKEN HERE> with the following secret Token key as shown below:

`https://cloud.iexapis.com/stable/stock/aapl/quote?token=`
`sk_5cfbd2112643432a9311436529774023`.

Enter the URL in a browser to check that everything is working as expected. The results should show the stock information, as shown in Figure 6-23.

Figure 6-23. *API results in browser*

Connect Watson with the Stock Market API via Cloud Functions

We described the step-by-step process to create a cloud function in the preceding topic. Let's create an action through IBM Cloud Functions to call the API.

Define the action, as shown in Figure 6-24.

1. Type your action name [action_name] (e.g., Stock-Connection).

2. Create a package under **Enclosing Package** with any [package_name] (e.g., Assistant-Function).

3. Select the **Runtime** language. In this example, we will use Node.js.

4. Click the **Create** button.

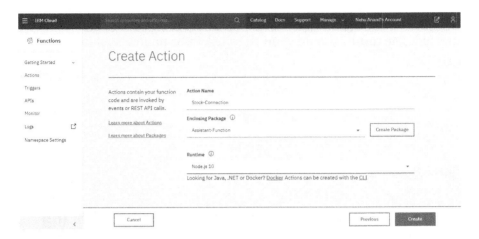

Figure 6-24. *IBM Cloud create Action page*

In your Cloud Functions actions, replace the existing code with the provided sample code.

This is a sample code. In the uri field, we are using the same API URL that we created earlier.

```
let rp = require('request-promise')
function main(params) {
    const options = {
        uri: "https://cloud.iexapis.com/stable/stock/" +
        encodeURIComponent(params.symbol) + "/quote?token=pk_
        1a5fa86b424845149eaddf14426b2d56" ,
        json: true
    }
    return rp(options)
    .then(res => {
        Stock_Price  = "Company Name : " + res.companyName + ",
        Open Price : " + res.open+ ", Close Price : " + res.
        close + ", Current Price : " + res.latestPrice + ",
        Low Value : "+ res.low + ", High Value : " + res.high
```

```
    return { Stock_Price
    }
})
}
```

We can now start editing the Stock-Connection function by replacing it with the preceding sample code in the Functions ➤ Actions ➤ Code console, as shown in Figure 6-25.

Figure 6-25. *IBM cloud function showing code snippet*

Now let's create the endpoint for this API call.

Go to **Endpoints**. Under **REST API**, copy and save the URL, as shown in Figure 6-26.

Figure 6-26. *Endpoints page*

Click **API-Key**. Copy and save the API key for later, as shown in Figure 6-27.

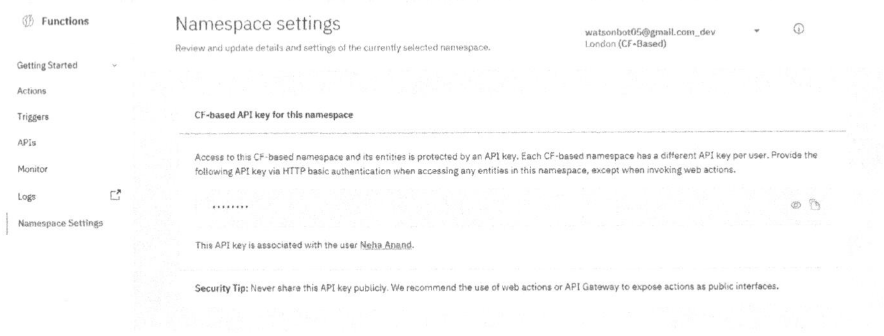

Figure 6-27. *Namespace settings page*

Now let's call this function in the skill created in the Watson Assistant service to fetch the result from the stock API and show the response in our bot.

Calling Cloud Function in Watson

You can download the skill JSON that has the use case configured for stock market data.

Go to the GitHub (https://github.com/watson05/Cognitive-Bot) to download Stock_Market.json.

Import it into the Watson Assistant service. We created a Watson Assistant-Virtual Bot in Chapter 4, so we'll use the same to import the downloaded skill. Let's look at importing a skill in the Watson Assistant service.

Go to your Watson Assistant service's Skill page.

1. Click **Create skill** and then select **Dialog skill**. Click **Create Dialog Skill**, which redirects to the Create Dialog Skill page.

2. In the top menu, select **Import skill**, as shown in Figure 6-28.

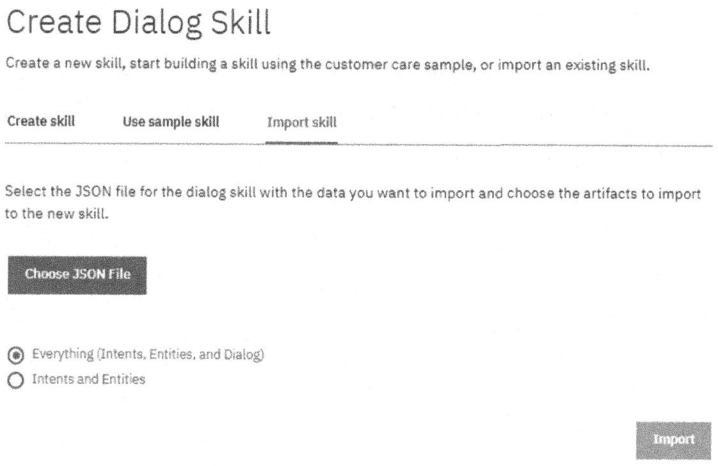

Create Dialog Skill

Create a new skill, start building a skill using the customer care sample, or import an existing skill.

Create skill   Use sample skill   Import skill

Select the JSON file for the dialog skill with the data you want to import and choose the artifacts to import to the new skill.

Choose JSON File

◉ Everything (Intents, Entities, and Dialog)
○ Intents and Entities

Import

Figure 6-28. *Import skil*

3. Click **Choose JSON File** and then browse. Select the JSON file that you downloaded and click **Import**, as shown in Figure 6-29.

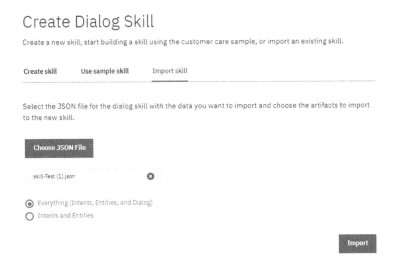

Figure 6-29. *Choose downloaded JSON file*

The skill is imported into the Watson Assistant service. You are redirected to the Dialog page, where you can see the Stock Market node configured, as shown in Figure 6-30.

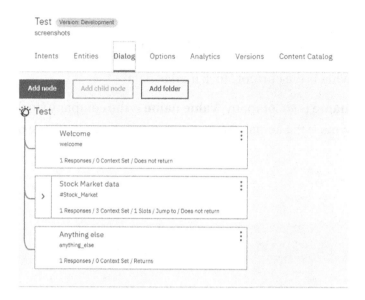

Figure 6-30. *Dialog page showing stock market data node*

Defining Components

Let's see how we have defined the following components for the Stock Market Data use case.

- **Intent Description:** Find the Stock Market Data

- **Intent Name: #Stock_Information**

- **Entity:** Company

- **Entity Values:** Company symbols such as AAPL, GOOGL, MSFT, and so on. We have added the symbol for 133 companies.

With this basic data populated, we need utterances or variations from end users that show how they would ask for this information.

- current stock price

- Tell me the current price of stocks.

- Tell me the stock price.

- What are the values of current stock?

- What is the current stock market data?

Entity name is @Company, **Value name** is the company stock symbol, and **Synonyms** is the actual company name, as shown in Figure 6-31.

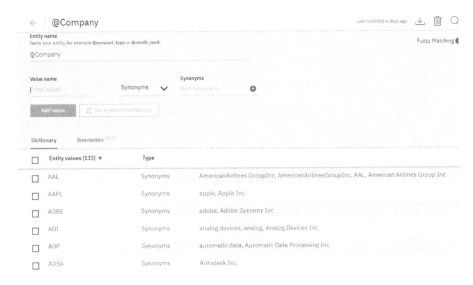

Figure 6-31. *Entity page*

Navigate to the Dialog section and click **Dialog**. Click the Stock Market Data node. You can see the intent defined as #Stock_Market. We defined the slots for checking whether the company name is mentioned in the query statement or not. If it is mentioned, then we move to the next step, which calls the API. If it is not mentioned, then we ask for the company name, as shown in Figure 6-32.

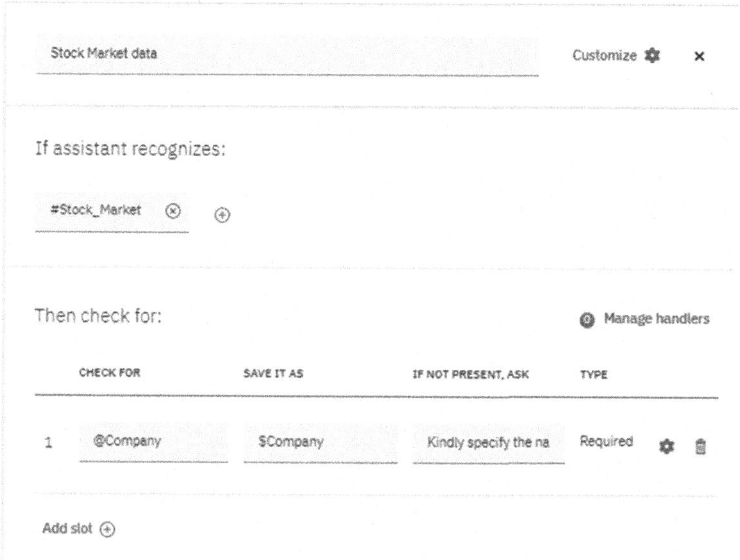

Stock Market data   Customize ⚙   ✕

If assistant recognizes:

#Stock_Market   ⊗   ⊕

Then check for: ⊚ Manage handlers

	CHECK FOR	SAVE IT AS	IF NOT PRESENT, ASK	TYPE		
1	@Company	$Company	Kindly specify the na	Required	⚙	🗑

Add slot ⊕

Figure 6-32. *Dialog node with information*

Calling the API

You have saved the company captured in a $symbol context variable, which is passed in the API. We are using the cloud function URL and API key from the cloud function. Refer to the API key that you copied earlier.

Enter the company name in the **$symbol** context variable that will be passed in the cloud function as a parameter. Paste the copied API key in the **$credentials** context variable, as shown in Figure 6-33. The JSON will be automatically generated, as shown in the following JSON sample.

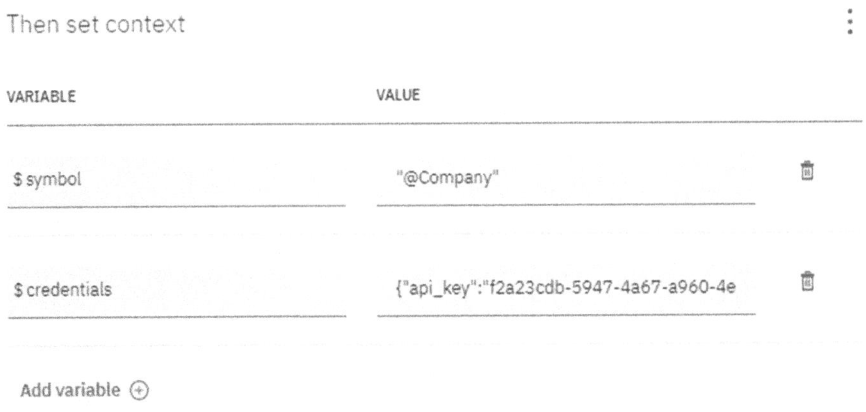

Then set context   ⋮

VARIABLE	VALUE	
$ symbol	"@Company"	🗑
$ credentials	{"api_key":"f2a23cdb-5947-4a67-a960-4e	🗑

Add variable ⊕

Figure 6-33. *Set context variable*

The following is the sample JSON that we are using to call the cloud function.

```
{
  "output": {
    "text": {
      "values": [],
      "selection_policy": "sequential"
}
  },
  "actions": [
    {
      "name": "/watsonbot05%40gmail.com_dev/Assistant-Function/
      Stock_Function",
      "type": "cloud_function",
      "parameters": {
        "symbol": "<? $Company ?>"
      },
```

```
      "credentials": "$credentials",
      "result_variable": "$response"
    }
  ],
  "context": {
    "symbol": "@Company",
    "credentials": {
      "api_key": "f2a23cdb-5947-4a67-a960-4eef2a9d2a5d:dfXh7zrB
      UgXqkG51zTGmL3gaXUi57KToRgG7HAOx8qWbgmbOU4E1UcMo7Aul2Hh6"
    }
  }
}
```

We'll call the cloud function in the JSON editor by clicking **Open JSON editor** in the **Then set context** menu.

Replace the code in the JSON editor, as shown in Figure 6-34.

Figure 6-34. *Open the JSON editor*

For the actions section in JSON, you need a part of your cloud function URL, which should look similar. The below is available in the Cloud Functions, Endpoint, API Key as a URL:

`https://eu-gb.functions.cloud.ibm.com/api/v1/namespaces/` `watsonbot05%40gmail.com_dev/actions/Assistant-Function/Stock-` `Connection`

We need to edit two sections from information from the Cloud Functions.

"name": "/watsonbot05%40gmail.com_dev/Assistant-Function/Stock-Connection" as shown in Figure 6-34.

Use the copied cloud function API key to api_key value. "api_key": `f2a23cdb-5947-4a67-a960-4eef2a9d2a5d:dfXh7zrBUgXqkG51zTGmL3gaXU` `i57KToRgG7HAOx8qWbgmbOU4E1UcMo7Aul2Hh6`

We have called the stock market API with a company symbol parameter. Now we need to show the result fetched from the API. For this, we have added a child node with a jump to the response from the parent node, as shown in Figure 6-35 and Figure 6-36.

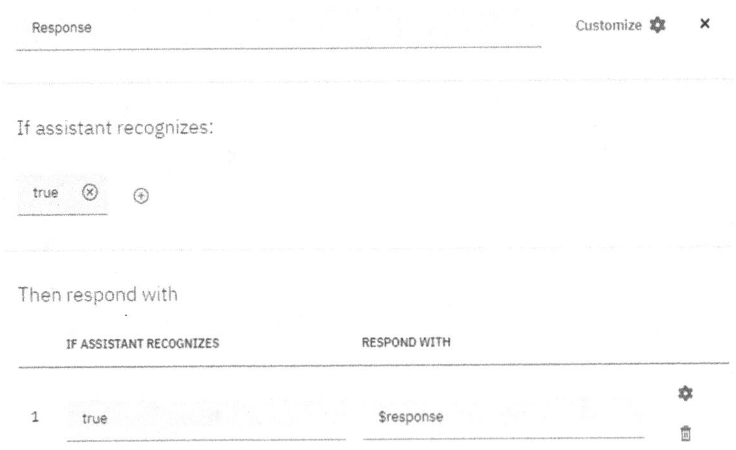

Figure 6-35. Child node to capture the response from API

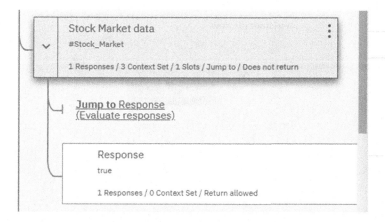

Figure 6-36. *Jump to Response*

We have fetched the response from the API in a $response context variable, which is mentioned in "result_variable" (see Figure 6-37).

```
1  {
2    "output": {
3      "text": {
4        "values": [],
5        "selection_policy": "sequential"
6      }
7    },
8    "actions": [
9      {
10       "name": "/watsonbot05%40gmail.com_dev/Assistant-Function/Stock_Function",
11       "type": "cloud_function",
12       "parameters": {
13         "symbol": "<? $Company ?>"
14       },
15       "credentials": "$credentials",
16       "result_variable": "$response"
17     }
```

Figure 6-37. *JSON showing result_variable*

Now let's try our use case on the bot. Link the skill with the bot, as you did earlier in the chapter. Try the use case to see the result of the company's stock market data, as shown in Figures 6-38 and 6-39.

Figure 6-38. *Testing use case in the bot*

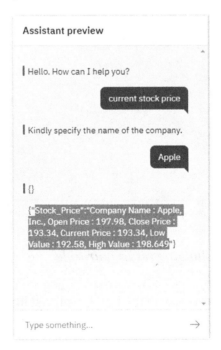

Figure 6-39. *Results shown*

Integrating with the Weather API

This use case describes how to integrate the Watson Assistant with a weather API. The user can ask weather-related questions. The bot responds to the questions by determining the weather condition or the temperature at a particular location.

Open Source Weather API

Go to `https://home.openweathermap.org` to get an open source weather API.

Click the **Sign Up** button to complete the registration, as shown in Figure 6-40.

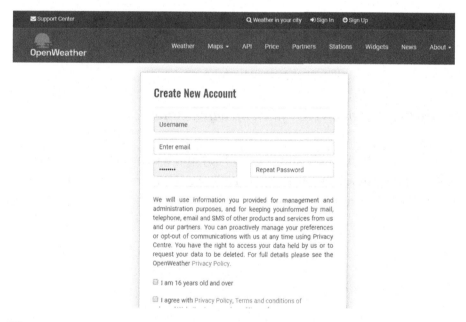

Figure 6-40. *Sign Up page*

Enter the required information to create an account, as shown in Figure 6-41.

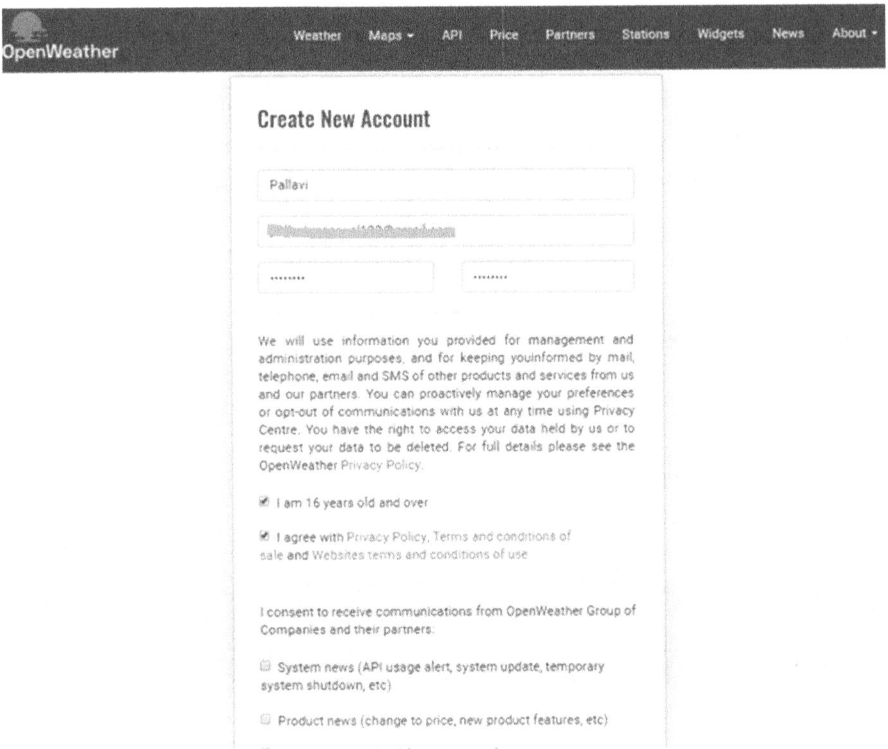

Figure 6-41. *Sign up page filled up with details*

A confirmation email with your API key and technical instructions is sent to the registered email address, as shown in Figure 6-42. Please note that it takes up to two hours to activate the API key.

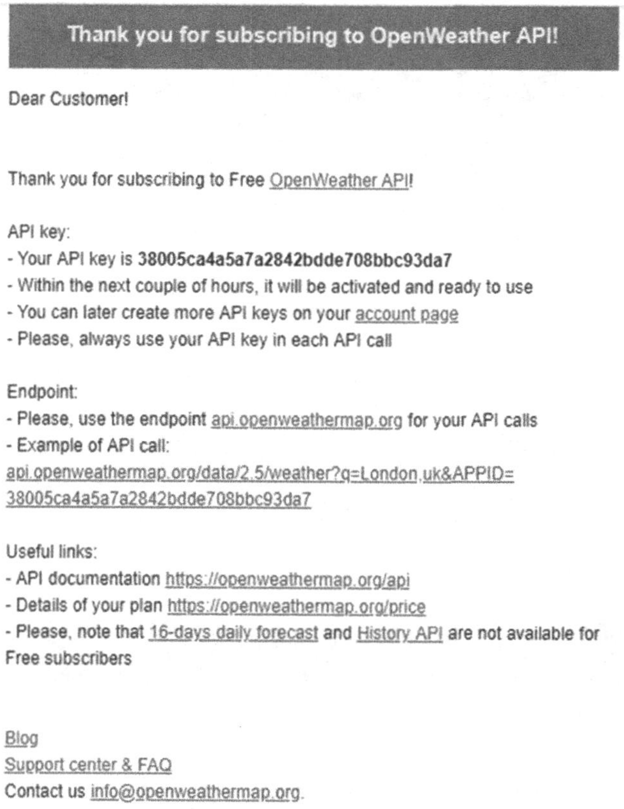

Thank you for subscribing to OpenWeather API!

Dear Customer!

Thank you for subscribing to Free OpenWeather API!

API key:
- Your API key is **38005ca4a5a7a2842bdde708bbc93da7**
- Within the next couple of hours, it will be activated and ready to use
- You can later create more API keys on your account page
- Please, always use your API key in each API call

Endpoint:
- Please, use the endpoint api.openweathermap.org for your API calls
- Example of API call:
api.openweathermap.org/data/2.5/weather?q=London,uk&APPID=
38005ca4a5a7a2842bdde708bbc93da7

Useful links:
- API documentation https://openweathermap.org/api
- Details of your plan https://openweathermap.org/price
- Please, note that 16-days daily forecast and History API are not available for
Free subscribers

Blog
Support center & FAQ
Contact us info@openweathermap.org.

Figure 6-42. *Email verification page*

As a next step, go to an API tab to check the freely available weather API doc, as shown in Figure 6-43 and Figure 6-44.

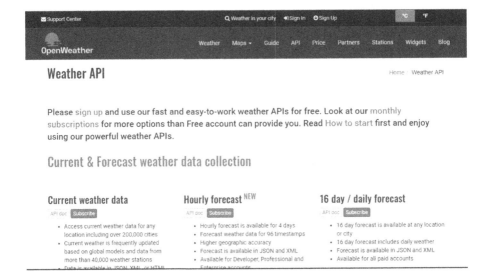

Figure 6-43. *Weather APIs*

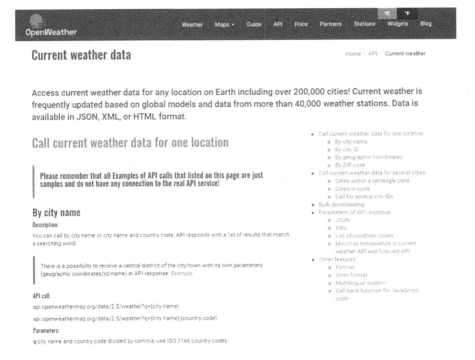

Figure 6-44. *Weather APIs*

You can check this URL through a browser. It shows the weather forecast, as shown in Figure 6-45.

In this case, we are using the URL to call the API by using the city name: http://api.openweathermap.org/data/2.5/weather?q=DELHI&un its=metric&APPID=19e8588cb3d7d0623e3a5a8ec529232f.

Figure 6-45. *API results in a browser*

Connecting Watson Assistant with the Weather API via Cloud Functions

We have already described the step-by-step process to create a cloud function. Let's create an action through IBM Cloud Functions to call the API.

Define the cloud function's create action, as shown in Figure 6-46.

1. Type your Action name [action_name] (e.g., Weather-Connection).

2. Create a package with any [package_name] (e.g., Assistant-Functions).

3. Select the **Runtime** language. In this example, we will use Node.js.

4. Click the **Create** button.

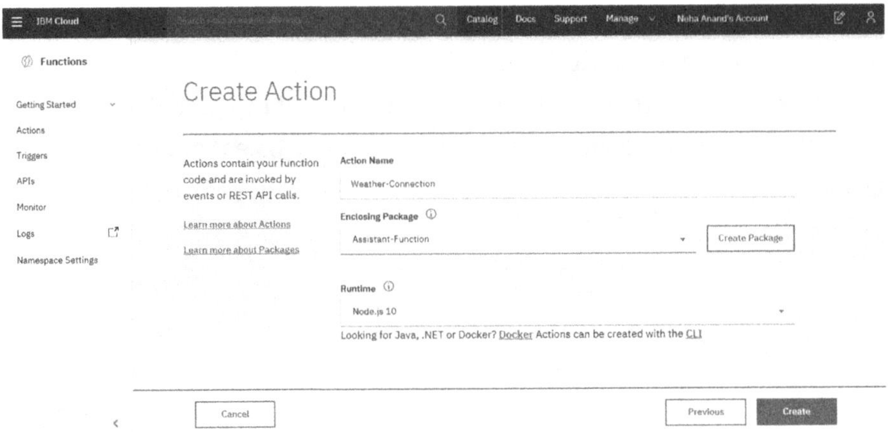

Figure 6-46. *IBM Cloud Create Action page*

In your Cloud Functions actions, replace the existing code with the provided sample code.

This is sample code, and in the uri field, we are using same API URL that we have created earlier.

```
let rp = require('request-promise')
function main(params) {
    const options = {
        uri: "http://api.openweathermap.org/data/2.5/weather?q="
        + encodeURIComponent(params.object_of_interest)+
        "&units=metric&APPID=19e8588cb3d7d0623e3a5a8ec529232f" ,
        json: true
    }
    return rp(options)
    .then(res => {
        WeatherReport = "Current Temperature : " +res.main.
        temp+ ", Pressure : " + res.main.pressure + ", Humidity
        : " + res.main.humidity + ", temp_min : " + res.main.
        temp_min + " , temp_max : " + res.main.temp_max
```

```
        return { WeatherReport
        }
    })
}
```

You can now start editing the Weather-Connection function by replacing with the preceding sample code in the Functions ä Actions ä Code console, as shown in Figure 6-47.

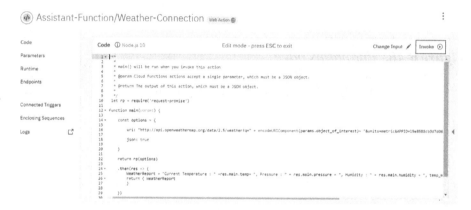

Figure 6-47. *IBM cloud function code snippet*

You have saved the credentials so that you can use them in Watson Assistant later.

Go to **Endpoints**. Under REST API, copy and save the URL, as shown in Figure 6-48.

Figure 6-48. *Endpoints page*

Copy and save the API key, as shown in Figure 6-49.

Figure 6-49. *Namespace settings page*

Now let's call this function in the skill created in the Watson Assistant service to fetch the result from the weather API, and show the response on our bot.

Calling Cloud Functions in Watson

You can download the skill JSON that has the use case configured for weather.

Go to GitHub (`https://github.com/watson05/Cognitive-Bot`) to download Weather.json.

Import the downloaded skill in the Watson Assistant service as explained in the Stock Market Data use case.

Once you have imported the skill, you are directed to the Dialog page, where you can see the Weather use case configured, as shown in Figure 6-50.

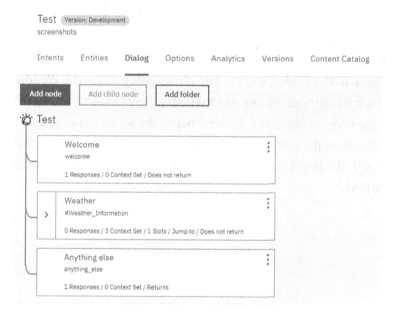

Figure 6-50. *Dialog page*

Let's look at how we have defined the following components for this use case.

- **Intent Description:** Find the weather of a location

- **Intent Name: #Weather_Information**

- **Entity:** @sys-location (System entity)

With this basic data populated, we need utterances or variations from end users on how they would ask for this information.

- How is the weather in <location>?

- What is the weather like today?

- Tell me about the weather.

- What is the weather forecast for <location>?

We have defined the entity as @sys-location since we want to extract the country, state, and city names from the user input.

Navigate to the Dialog section and click **Dialog**. Click the Weather node. You see the intent defined as #Weather_Information. We have defined the slots for checking the weather in the location mentioned in the query statement. If it is mentioned, then we move to the next step, which calls the API. If it is not mentioned, then we ask for the location, as shown in Figure 6-51.

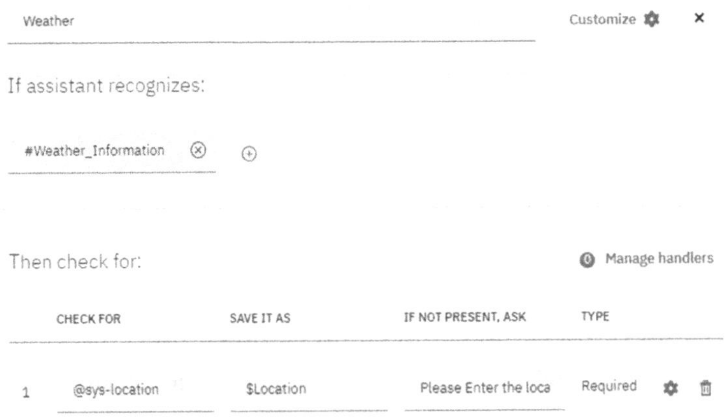

Figure 6-51. *Dialog node with information*

Calling the API

You have saved the location captured in a $Location context variable, which is passed in the API. We are using the cloud function URL and API key from the cloud function.

Enter the location name in the **$location** context variable, which is passed in the cloud function as a parameter. Paste the copied API key in the **$credentials** context variable, as shown in Figure 6-52. The JSON is automatically generated, as shown in the sample JSON.

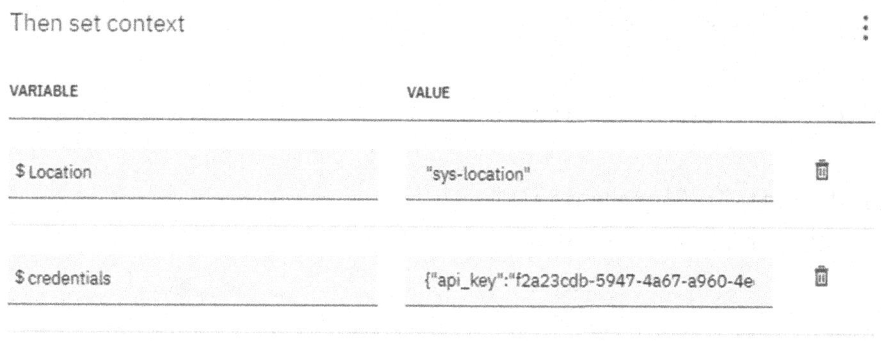

Figure 6-52. *Set context variable*

The following is the sample JSON that we are using to call the cloud function.

```
{
"context": {
"credentials": {
"api_key": "f2a23cdb-5947-4a67-a960-4eef2a9d2a5d:dfXh7zrBUgXqkG
51zTGmL3gaXUi57KToRgG7HAOx8qWbgmbOU4E1UcMo7Aul2Hh6"
},
"object_of_interest": "@object_of_interest"
},
```

```
"output": {
"text": {
"values": [],
"selection_policy": "sequential"
}
},
"actions": [
{
"name": "/watsonbot05%40gmail.com_dev/Assistant-Function/
Weather-Connection",
"type": "cloud_function",
"parameters": {
"object_of_interest": "$Location"
},
"credentials": "$credentials",
"result_variable": "$response"
}
]
}
```

We'll call the cloud function in the JSON editor by clicking **Open JSON editor** in the **Then set context** the hamburger menu.

Replace the code in the JSON editor, as shown in Figure 6-53.

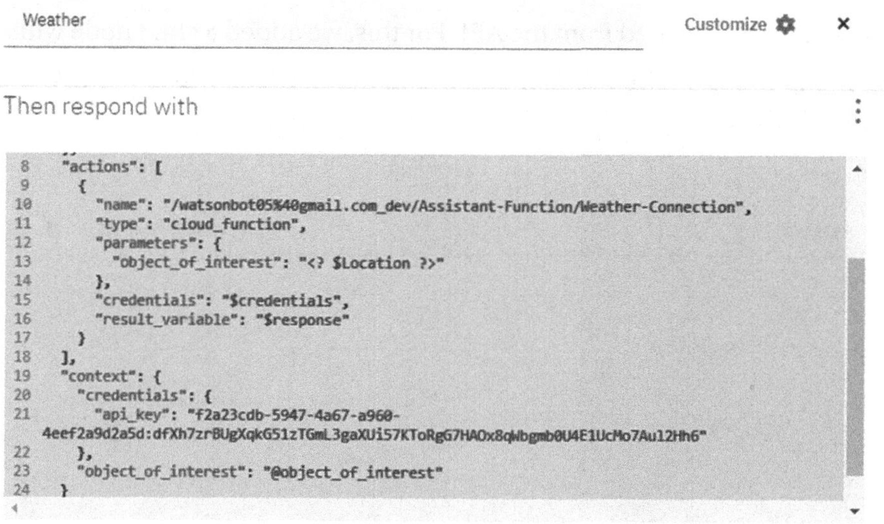

Figure 6-53. *Open JSON editor*

For the actions section in JSON, you need part of your cloud function URL, which should look similar to this. The following is available in the Cloud Functions, Endpoint, API Key as a URL:

`https://eu-gb.functions.cloud.ibm.com/api/v1/namespaces/watsonbot05%40gmail.com_dev/actions/Assistant-Function/Weather-Connection`

We need to edit two sections from information from the Cloud Functions.

"name": "/watsonbot05%40gmail.com_dev/Assistant-Function/Weather-Connection "as shown in Figure 6-53.

To hand over the credentials in the context, use the copied cloud function API key to api_key value. "api_key": `"f2a23cdb-5947-4a67-a960-4eef2a9d2a5d:dfXh7zrBUgXqkG51zTGmL3gaXUi57KToRgG7HAOx8qWbgmbOU4E1UcMo7Aul2Hh6"`.

We called the weather API with a location parameter. Now we need to show the result fetched from the API. For this, we added a child node with the jump to response from the parent node, as shown in Figure 6-54 and Figure 6-55.

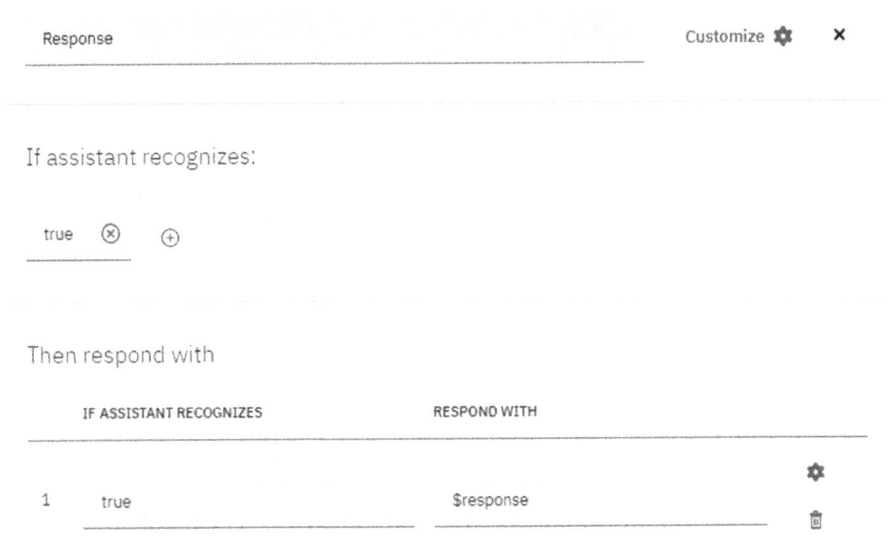

Response   Customize ⚙   ✕

If assistant recognizes:

true   ⊗   ⊕

Then respond with

	IF ASSISTANT RECOGNIZES	RESPOND WITH	
1	true	$response	⚙ 🗑

Figure 6-54. *Child node to capture the response from API*

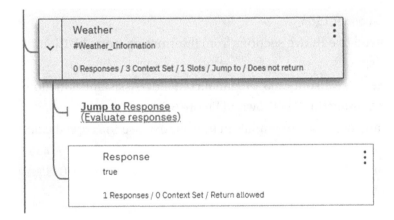

Figure 6-55. *Jump to Response*

We fetched the response from the API in a $response context variable mentioned in the "result_variable" (see Figure 6-56).

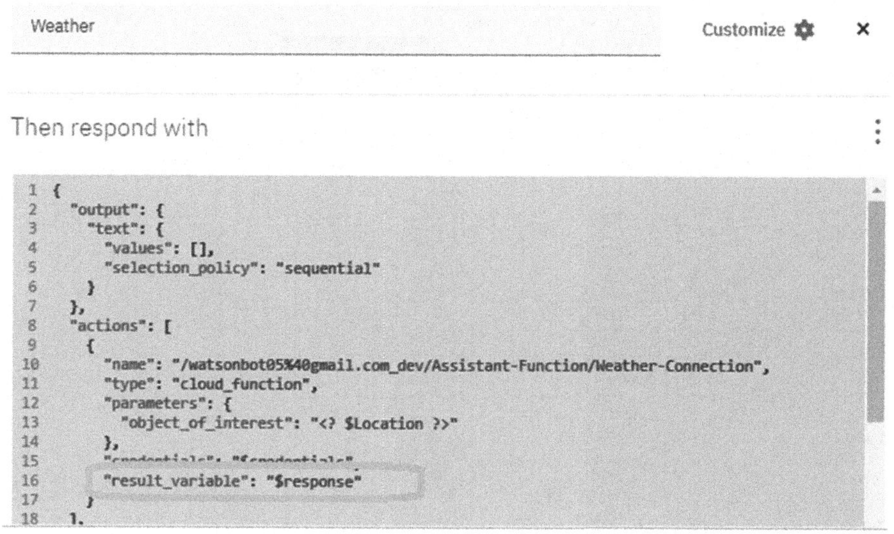

Weather   Customize ⚙   ✕

Then respond with   ⋮

```
1  {
2     "output": {
3        "text": {
4           "values": [],
5           "selection_policy": "sequential"
6        }
7     },
8     "actions": [
9        {
10          "name": "/watsonbot05%40gmail.com_dev/Assistant-Function/Weather-Connection",
11          "type": "cloud_function",
12          "parameters": {
13             "object_of_interest": "<? $Location ?>"
14          },
15          "credentials": "$credentials"
16          "result_variable": "$response"
17       }
18    ]
```

Figure 6-56. *JSON showing result_variable*

Now let's try our use case in the bot. Link the skill with the bot as you did earlier in the chapter. Try the use case to see the weather forecast, as shown in Figure 6-57 and Figure 6-58.

Figure 6-57. *Testing the use case in the bot*

Figure 6-58. Results shown

Conclusion

This concludes the chapter on the various types of use cases that we can develop using the IBM Watson platform to integrate with third-party APIs and further enrich our bot's conversation quality. We created ready-to-use use cases for investment planning, stock market information, and the weather in a particular location.

CHAPTER 7

Integrating with Advance Services

This chapter describes the integration of Watson Assistant with built-in advanced IBM services, such as the Tone Analyzer service and the Watson Discovery service. We also cover integration with other messaging platforms, such as Facebook Messenger and Slack.

Facebook Messenger Integration with IBM Watson Assistant

Let's discuss how the Watson conversation service is integrated with chat platforms such as Facebook Messenger and Slack. It provides the process for designing and running the bots that live inside messaging platforms, such as Slack, Facebook, and Twilio.

Let's integrate Facebook Messenger with IBM Watson in a previously configured use case.

Creating a Page on Facebook

First, let's create a page on Facebook in which we will integrate with the IBM Watson Assistant by using the following steps.

1. Log in to your Facebook account.

© Navin Sabharwal, Sudipta Barua, Neha Anand, Pallavi Aggarwal 2020
N. Sabharwal et al., *Developing Cognitive Bots Using the IBM Watson Engine*,
https://doi.org/10.1007/978-1-4842-5555-1_7

2. Click the **Create** button and select the **Page** option, as shown in Figure 7-1.

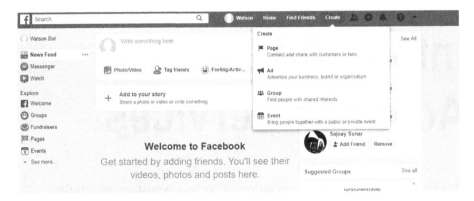

Figure 7-1. *Welcome to Facebook*

3. Under the Create page, select the community or public section and click Get Started.

4. Fill in the required information. We named our page Chat Utility, as shown in Figure 7-2.

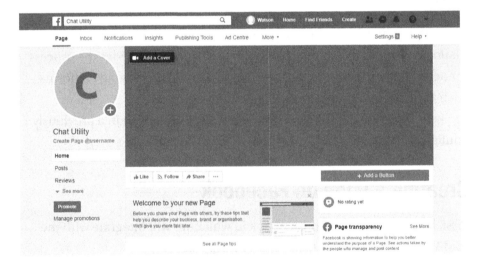

Figure 7-2. *Facebook Chat Utility page*

5. Go to `http://developers.facebook.com` and log in with your Facebook credentials. You are redirected to the page shown in Figure 7-3.

Figure 7-3. *Facebook for developer page*

6. Select **Create App** under the **My Apps** drop-down menu.

7. Create a new app ID by entering information in **Display Name** and **Contact** (e.g., Display Name: Customer Service app and Contact Email: xxxxxxxxxx@xxxxx), as shown in Figure 7-4.

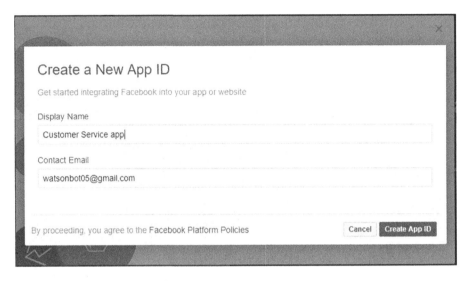

Figure 7-4. *Creation of new app ID*

8.   And click the **Create APP ID** button.

9.   Once the new app ID has been created, you are redirected to the Facebook app page, as shown in Figure 7-5.

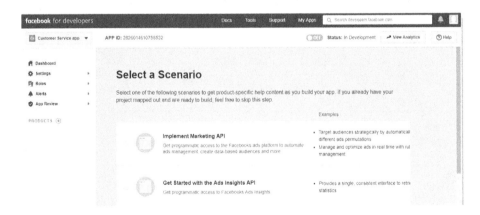

Figure 7-5. *Facebook app page*

10. In the navigation pane, select the **Settings** tab and choose **Basic**. Under the App Secret option, click **Show**.

11. Click the **App Secret** code and copy the app secret key that is used in Watson Assistant, as shown in Figure 7-6.

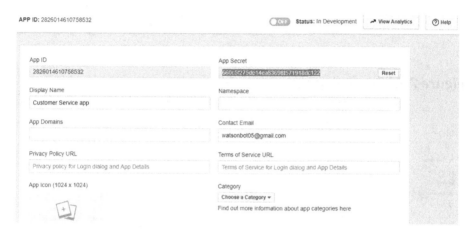

Figure 7-6. *App Secret Key*

12. Navigate back to the Facebook app page, and click the plus sign (+) next to **Products** on the left navigation pane.

13. Under **Add a product**, find the **Messenger** tile and click the **Set Up** button, as shown in Figure 7-7. You are redirected to the page shown in Figure 7-8.

Figure 7-7. *Products page*

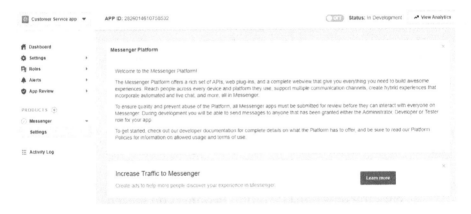

Figure 7-8. *Messenger Platform page*

14. In the Messenger settings, scroll down to **Token Generation**.

15. Click **Select a Page** from the drop-down menu and choose the newly created Facebook page.

16. Copy the **Page Access Token**, which will be used in Watson Assistant (see Figure 7-9).

Access Tokens

Generate a Page access token to start using the platform APIs. You will be able to generate an access token for a Page if:

1. You are one of the Page admins, and
2. The app has been granted the Page's permission to manage and access Page conversations in Messenger.

Note: If your app is in dev mode, you can still generate a token but will only be able to access people who manage the app or Page.

Page	Page Access Token	
Chat Utility ▼	EAAoKPs0BG4QBAB8JT2t9PMdUj16kZAgvsxBW6teeZB4c6hda3FRgO3jHNSGwHOVVDLePdKmHCB8D	**Edit Permissions**
Create a new page		

Figure 7-9. *Page Access Token*

Let's move to the IBM Watson console and integrate the Watson Assistant.

1. After logging in to the IBM Cloud, launch the AI service created in Chapter 6.

2. Select the skill in which you want to integrate with Facebook Messenger. Click the **Skills** button and then click **test**, as shown in Figure 7-10.

Assistants Skills		Instance Watson Assistant-Virtual Bot
My first assistant Built for you to explore and learn.	Skills (0)	Integrations (0) ⋮
test	Skills (1)	Integrations (1) ⋮ ⊖
Virtual Bot Bot featuring with BFSI, IT, Weather, Stock	Skills (1) Test	Integrations (2) ⋮ ● ⊖

Figure 7-10. *Watson Assistant Skill page*

3. Click the **Add Integration** button. Select **Facebook Messenger** under **Third-party integrations**, as shown in Figure 7-11.

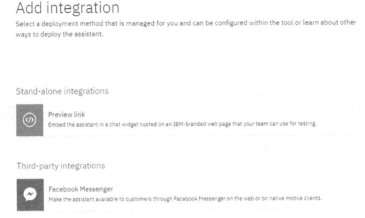

Figure 7-11. *Add Integration page*

4. Enter the required information in **Name** and
    Description on the Facebook Messenger Integration
    page, as shown in Figure 7-12.

Figure 7-12. *Configuration for Facebook Messenger*

5. Paste the copied **App Secret Key** into the
    Application secret field, as shown in Figure 7-13.

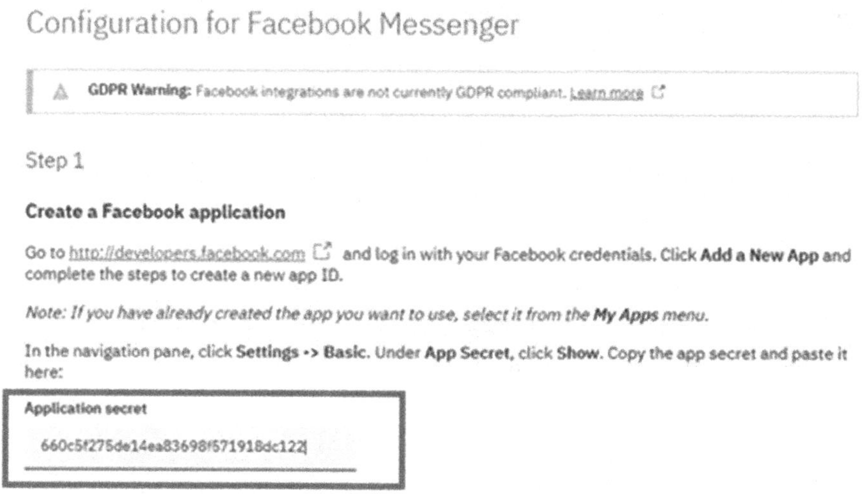

Configuration for Facebook Messenger

⚠ **GDPR Warning:** Facebook integrations are not currently GDPR compliant. Learn more ☐

Step 1

Create a Facebook application

Go to http://developers.facebook.com ☐ and log in with your Facebook credentials. Click **Add a New App** and complete the steps to create a new app ID.

Note: If you have already created the app you want to use, select it from the **My Apps** menu.

In the navigation pane, click **Settings** -> **Basic**. Under **App Secret**, click **Show**. Copy the app secret and paste it here:

Application secret

660c5f275de14ea83698f571918dc122

Figure 7-13. *Watson Assistant Facebook Messenger Configuration page*

6. Paste the copied Page access token under **Page Access token**, as shown in Figure 7-14.

7. Copy the **Generated verify token**, which will be used to verify your webhook URL.

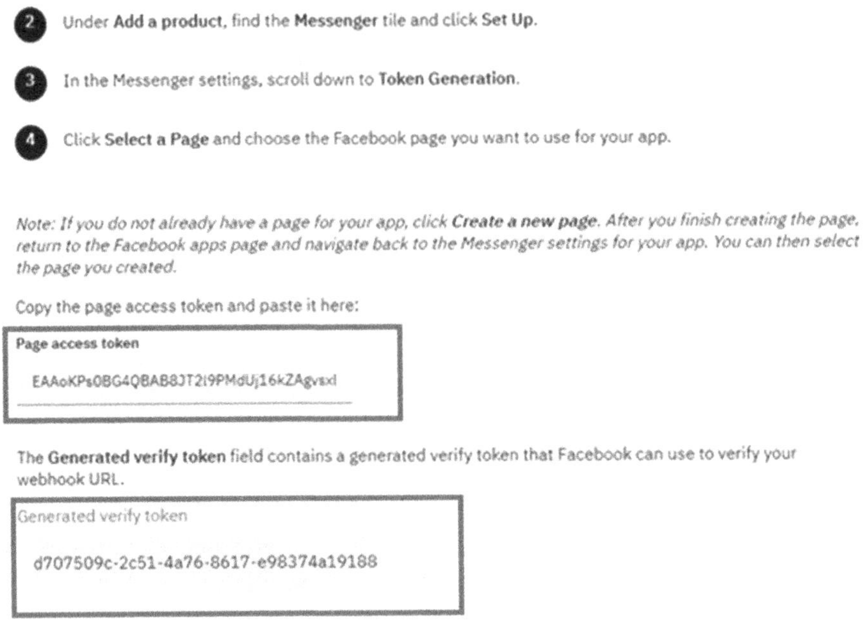

2 Under **Add a product**, find the **Messenger** tile and click **Set Up**.

3 In the Messenger settings, scroll down to **Token Generation**.

4 Click **Select a Page** and choose the Facebook page you want to use for your app.

*Note: If you do not already have a page for your app, click **Create a new page**. After you finish creating the page, return to the Facebook apps page and navigate back to the Messenger settings for your app. You can then select the page you created.*

Copy the page access token and paste it here:

> **Page access token**
>
> EAAoKPsOBG4QBAB8JT2i9PMdUj16kZAgvsxl

The **Generated verify token** field contains a generated verify token that Facebook can use to verify your webhook URL.

> Generated verify token
>
> d707509c-2c51-4a76-8617-e98374a19188

Figure 7-14. *Page access token and Generated verify token*

8. Under **Configure Facebook webhooks** on **the** Facebook Messenger Integration page, click **Generate callback URL**, as shown in Figure 7-15.

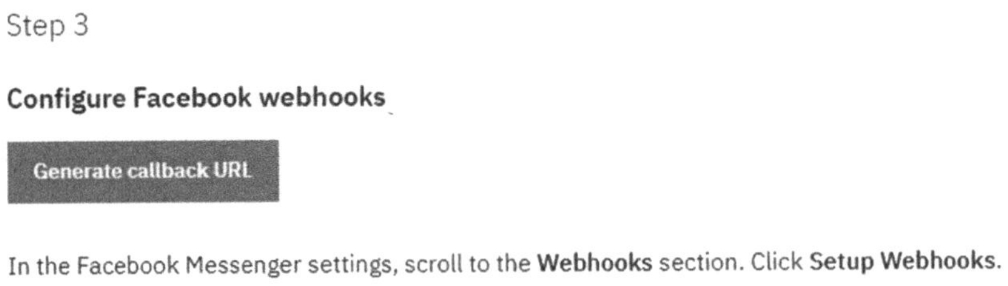

Step 3

Configure Facebook webhooks

> **Generate callback URL**

In the Facebook Messenger settings, scroll to the **Webhooks** section. Click **Setup Webhooks**.

Figure 7-15. *Generate callback URL*

9. Once the callback URL has been generated, it is shown
    under **Generate callback URL** on the Facebook
    Messenger Integration page (see Figure 7-16).

10. Copy the **Generate callback URL**.

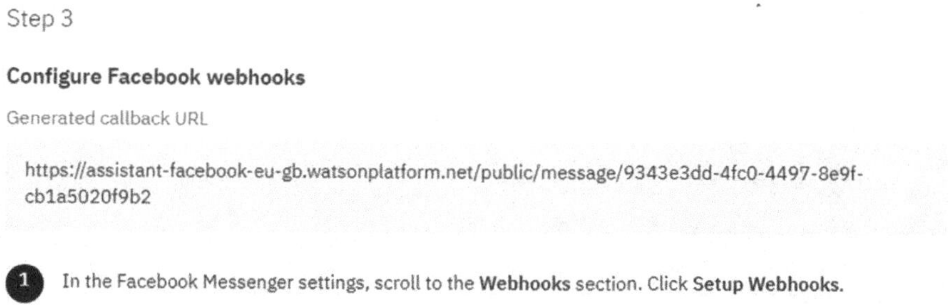

Step 3

Configure Facebook webhooks

Generated callback URL

https://assistant-facebook-eu-gb.watsonplatform.net/public/message/9343e3dd-4fc0-4497-8e9f-
cb1a5020f9b2

 In the Facebook Messenger settings, scroll to the **Webhooks** section. Click **Setup Webhooks**.

Figure 7-16. *Generated callback URL*

11. Go back to the Facebook App page. In the Facebook
    Messenger settings, scroll to the Webhooks section.

12. Click **Subscribe to Events**.

13. In the New Page Subscription window, insert the
    copied Generated callback URL into the **Callback
    URL** field. Insert the copied Generated verify token
    into the **Verify token** field.

14. In the Subscription field, select **messages** and
    messaging_postbacks and click **Verify and Save**, as
    shown in Figure 7-17.

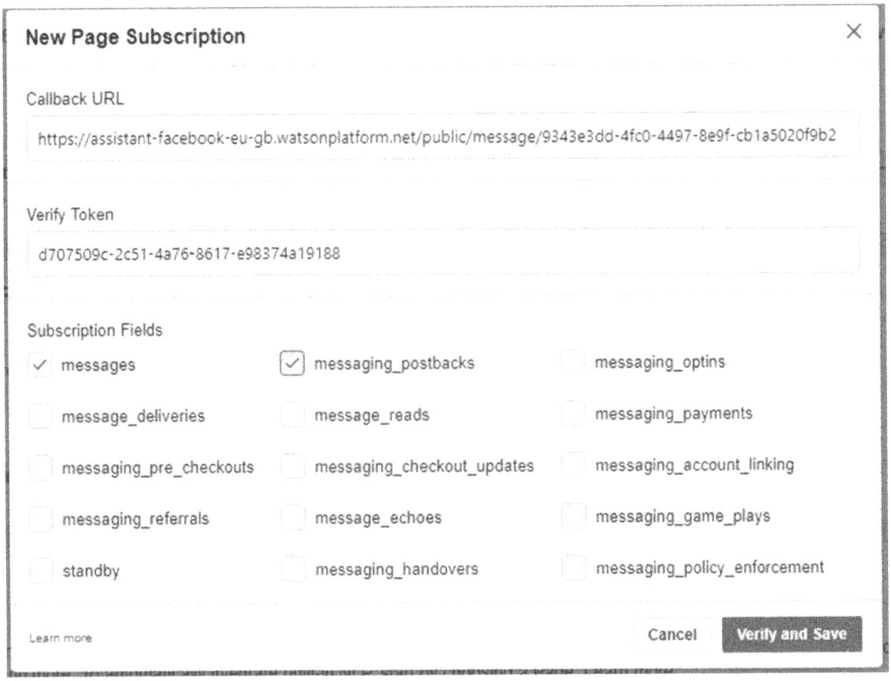

Figure 7-17. *New page subscription*

15. In the Messenger settings on the Facebook app page, go to the **Webhooks** section and click **Select a page**. Select the same Facebook page as in the previous step.

16. Click the **Subscribe** button, as shown in Figure 7-18.

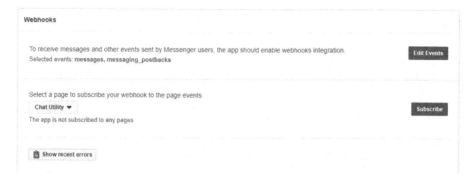

Figure 7-18. *Webhooks on Facebook App page*

At this point, you have completed all the steps required to integrate Watson Assistant with Facebook Messenger. Now, let's test our integration scenario.

1. Go to the Facebook page and click the **Send Message** button. Select **Test button**, as shown in Figure 7-19.

Figure 7-19. *Facebook page*

2. Test the skill that we integrated with Messenger. See the Weather use case scenario, as shown in Figure 7-20.

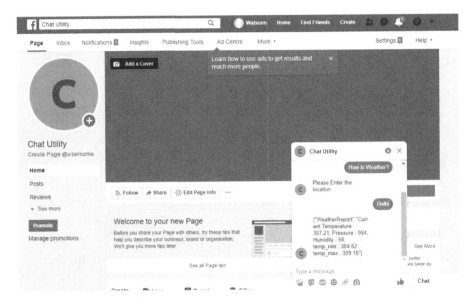

Figure 7-20. *Testing Use Case on Facebook page*

Using Other Advanced Watson Services

Watson Discovery Service

The Watson Discovery service enables you to rapidly ingest, normalize, enrich, index, and search your unstructured data. It simplifies the infrastructure, scale, and algorithm challenges associated with enriching and analyzing large datasets. It gives you the capability to produce data in multiple formats, including PDFs, Word docs, HTML, and JSON type files.

Figure 7-21. *Architecture of Watson Discovery service*

Watson Discovery takes only a few steps to analyze and summarize large unstructured data, create a query that provides the information you need, and then integrates these insights into a new application or existing solution.

IBM Watson Discovery brings together a functionally rich set of integrated, automated Watson APIs that do the following.

- Trains unstructured data. Upload your own document or crawl from Box, Salesforce, Microsoft SharePoint Online, IBM Cloud Object Storage, and Microsoft SharePoint 2016 data sources, or do a web crawl with the Discovery tooling. Discovery environment can hold multiple private collections. Each collection is paired with a configuration that tells Discovery how to upload and process the files. We can specify how to convert the different file types in the dataset and choose which natural processing enrichments to apply to each document text and how the resulting data should be cleaned and normalized.

- Group documents/data to be ingested, indexed, normalized, and ready to be queried. Enrichments applied to documents. The Entity Extraction, Sentiment Analysis, Category Classification, and Concept Tagging enrichments are automatically applied to the text field by Discovery through natural language understanding (NLU).

- Once the data has been enriched, builds a query to search information.

Let's take a deep dive into the Watson Discovery service to see how results are fetched from a data collection based on input query.

To set up a Watson Discovery service, go to the IBM Cloud Catalog page at https://cloud.ibm.com/catalog.

1. Search for **Discovery** and click the **Discovery**
   service, as shown in Figure 7-22.

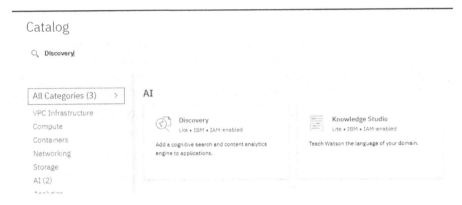

Figure 7-22. *Watson Catalog page*

2. Enter the required information in **Service name**
   ([Service_name], e.g. Discovery-Test) to create a
   service. Choose a region to deploy, as shown in
   Figure 7-23.

Figure 7-23. *Watson Discovery page*

3. Choose the **Lite** plan on the pricing plan page and
   click the **Create** button, as shown in Figure 7-24.

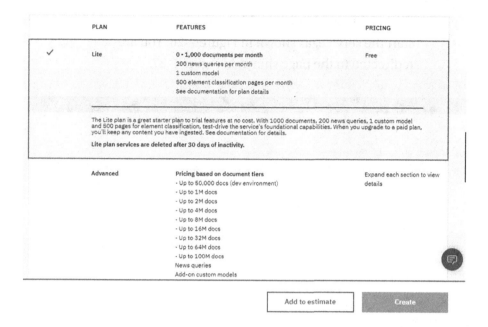

Figure 7-24. *Discovery service plan*

4. Once the service instance is created, it is shown in the Services section. Select the **Discovery-Test** service, as shown in Figure 7-25.

Figure 7-25. *Resource List*

5.   Click the **Launch Watson Discovery** button to start the service, as shown in Figure 7-26. You are redirected to the page shown in Figure 7-27.

Figure 7-26. Launch Watson Discovery

6.   On the Manage Data screen, create a data collection. Click the **Upload your own data** button and create a new private collection in Discovery.

7.   Enter the required information. The **Collection name** is **AI Data**. Select the language of your choice (English by default) and then click the **Create** button, as shown in Figure 7-28.

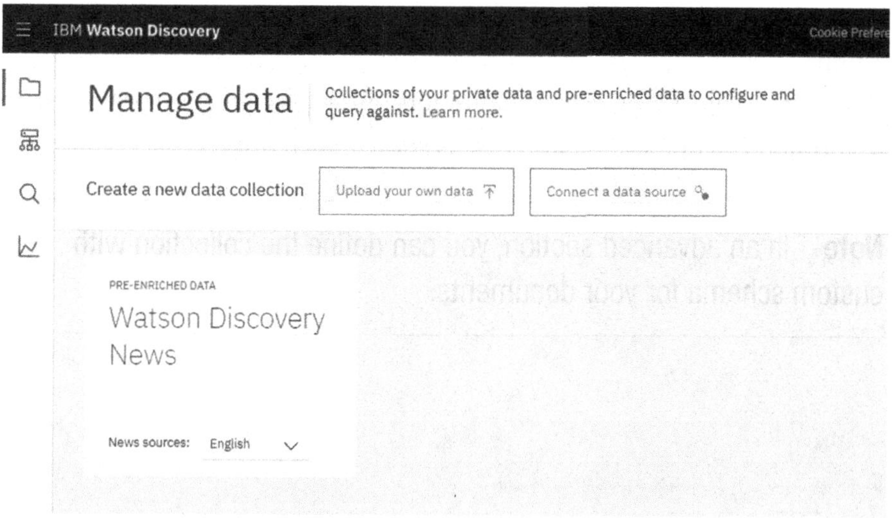

Figure 7-27. *IBM Watson Discovery page*

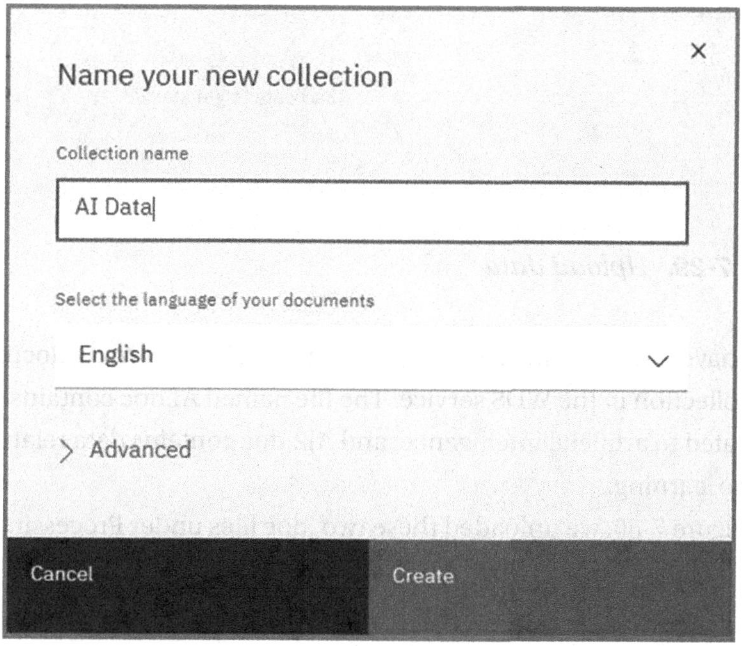

Figure 7-28. *Creation of collection*

Once the collection has been created, you need to upload data in this section.

You can drag and drop the documents into your collection or browse the computer to upload documents, as shown in Figure 7-29.

Note   In an advanced section, you can define the collection with custom schema for your documents.

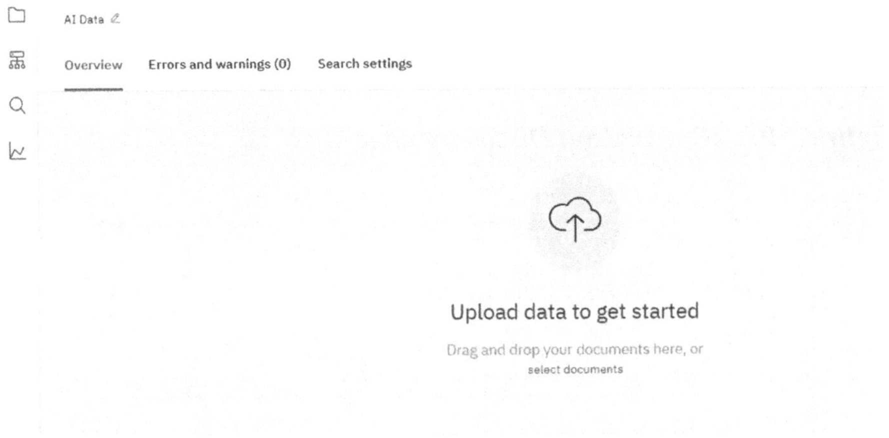

AI Data

Overview   Errors and warnings (0)   Search settings

Upload data to get started

Drag and drop your documents here, or
select documents

Figure 7-29. Upload data

We have added artificial intelligence and machine learning documents to the collection in the WDS service. The file named AI.doc contains data related to artificial intelligence, and AI2.doc contains data related to machine learning.

In Figure 7-30, we uploaded these two .doc files under Processing.

Figure 7-30. *Processing your data*

After the process is completed, the following information is displayed, as shown in Figure 7-31.

- The document count has increased to 2.

- The fields identified from your documents.

- Enrichments were applied to your documents. The Entity Extraction, Sentiment Analysis, Category Classification, and Concept Tagging enrichments are automatically applied to the text field by Discovery.

Figure 7-31. *Enrichments applied to document*

Now, let's run prebuilt queries, as shown on the right side of the page. Clicking the Run button as shown in Figure 7-32 redirects to the page shown in Figure 7-33.

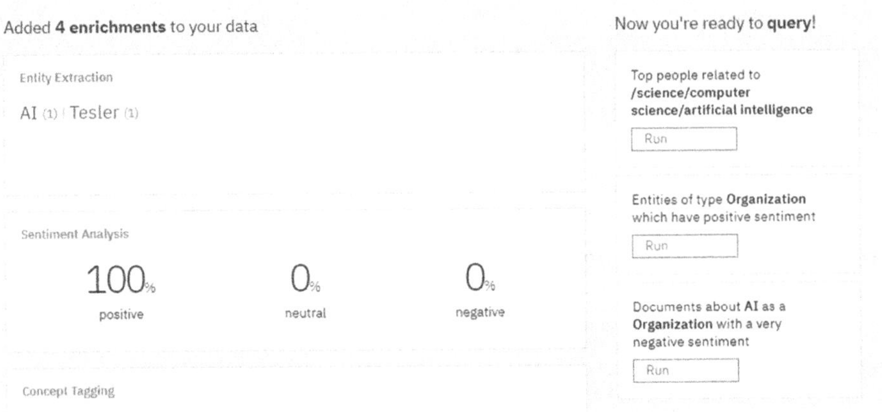

Added 4 enrichments to your data
Entity Extraction
AI (1) | Tesler (1)
Sentiment Analysis
100%
positive
0%
neutral
0%
negative
Concept Tagging
Now you're ready to query!
Top people related to /science/computer science/artificial intelligence
Run
Entities of type Organization which have positive sentiment
Run
Documents about AI as a Organization with a very negative sentiment
Run

***Figure 7-32.** Manage Data page*

AI Data / Build queries
Build a query using one or more of these components. Learn more.
Use a sample query
Search for documents
Build in visual mode
Use natural language
Use the Discovery Query Language
Include analysis of your results
Build in visual mode
Run query
Close
Train Watson to improve results
Summary
JSON
Passages

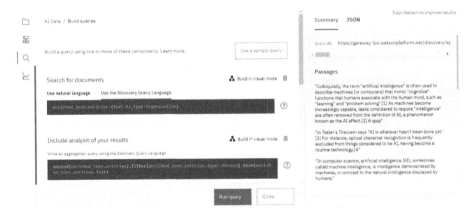

***Figure 7-33.** Build queries page*

Let's try a quick natural language query.

Enter your query under the **Use natural language** field. Click **Run query**.

The search results are shown on the right side of the screen. It extracts the data from all the documents matching the keywords as per the relevance using NLP, NLU, and machine learning, as shown in Figure 7-34.

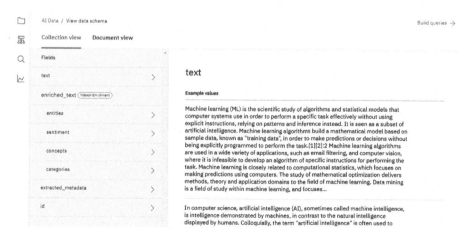

Figure 7-34. *Build queries page*

To see the schema of collections, go to **View data schema** and select the **Collection view** tab. The collection's data schema is shown. It contains text, enriched_text, entities, sentiment, and more, as shown in Figure 7-35.

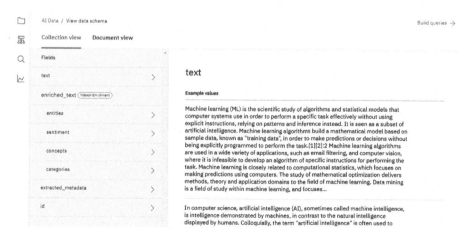

Figure 7-35. *View Data schema*

To connect the Watson Discovery service with our bot, let's create a search skill from the Skill page.

1. Go to the IBM Watson Assistant.

2. Select a search skill and click the **Next** button, as shown in Figure 7-36.

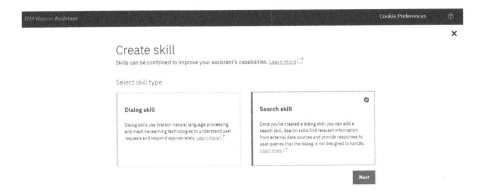

Figure 7-36. *Watson Assistant Create Skill page*

3. Fill in the required information for Name and Description. Click the Continue button, as shown in Figure 7-37.

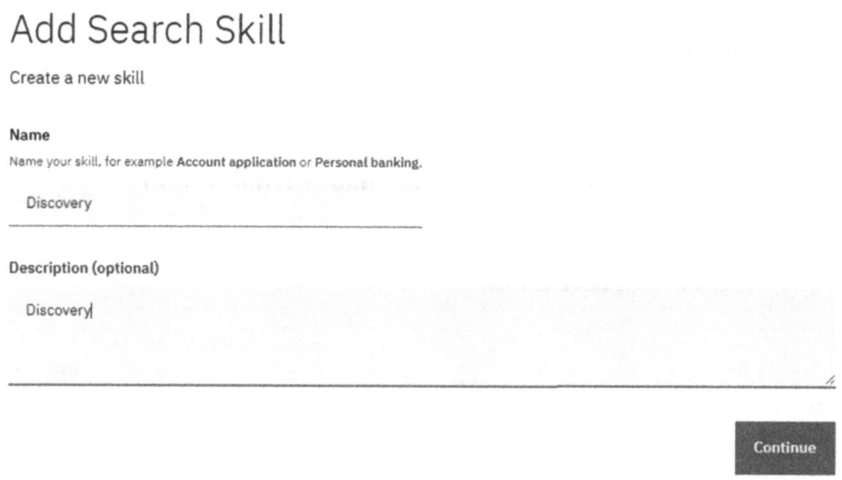

Add Search Skill

Create a new skill

Name

Name your skill, for example **Account application** or **Personal banking**.

Discovery

Description (optional)

Discovery

Continue

Figure 7-37. *Watson Assistant Add Search Skill page*

4. Once the skill is created, you need to choose the
   Discovery service instance to connect with the skill,
   and you need to select the collection that you want
   to use (e.g., Discovery instance: Discovery-Test and
   collection: AI Data), as shown in Figure 7-38.

5. Click the **Configure** button.

Figure 7-38. *Watson Assistant Search Skill page*

6. To configure the search response, map your data schema from Discovery to the title, body, and URL fields to define which results are shown to end users, as shown in Figure 7-39. For example, Title is mapped with extracted_metadata_filename, and Body is mapped with text.

7. Click the **Create** button.

Figure 7-39. *Configure Search Response*

Now the integration of WDS with the assistant is complete, so you can test your assistant with a query (What is machine learning?) by using the **Try it out** panel, as shown in Figure 7-40.

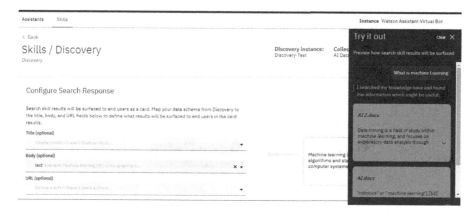

Figure 7-40.   *Try it out page*

Now let's try our use case in the bot. Link the skill with the assistant as was done earlier in the chapter, and try the use case to see the search results from WDS, as shown in Figure 7-41 and Figure 7-42.

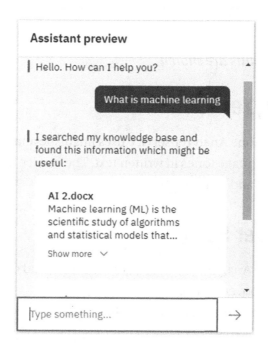

Figure 7-41.   *Testing the use case*

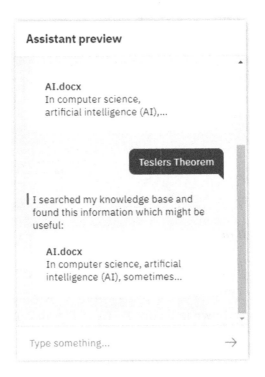

Figure 7-42.   *Results are shown*

Tone Analyzer

The IBM Watson Tone Analyzer service uses linguistic analysis to detect emotional and language tones in written text. The service can analyze tone at both document and sentence levels.

Tone Analyzer Service

To set up the Tone Analyzer Service, go to the IBM Cloud Catalog page at `https://cloud.ibm.com/catalog`.

Search for **Tone Analyzer**. Click the **Tone Analyzer** service, as shown in Figure 7-43.

Figure 7-43. *IBM Cloud Catalog page*

Enter the required information to create a service (e.g., [Service_name], Tone_Analyzer-Demo). Choose a region to deploy in and select the relevant tags, as shown in Figure 7-44.

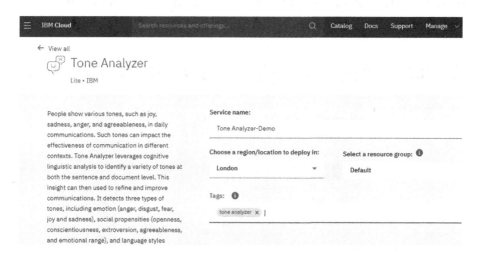

Figure 7-44. *IBM Cloud Tone Analyzer page*

Choose the Lite plan from the pricing plan page, as shown in Figure 7-45.

Figure 7-45. *Pricing plans*

Copy the credentials to authenticate your service instance.

On the Manage page, click **Show** to view your credentials. Copy the API Key and URL values so that you can use them in IBM Cloud Functions later, as shown in Figure 7-46.

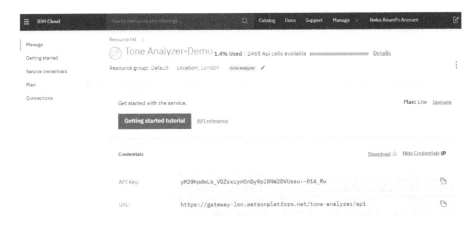

Figure 7-46. *Tone Analyzer Manage page*

Connecting Watson with Tone Analyzer Service via Cloud Functions

We have already covered the step-by-step process to create Cloud Functions. Let's create an action through Cloud Functions in IBM Cloud to call the API.

Creating an Action

Define the Cloud Functions action, as shown in Figure 7-47.

1. Type your Action name (e.g., [action_name], Tone-Analyzer).

2. Create a package under **Enclosing Package** with any [package_name] (e.g., Assistant-Function).

3. Select the **Runtime** language. In this example, we used Node.js.

4. Click the **Create** button.

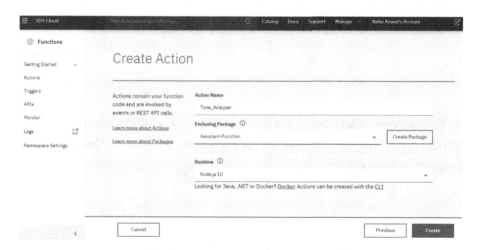

Figure 7-47. *IBM Cloud create Action page*

In your Cloud Functions actions, replace the existing sample code that is used to call the IBM Tone Analyzer service, as shown in Figure 7-48.

In the **url** field and the **iam_apikey** field, replace the same URL and API key that you copied while creating the Tone Analyzer service.

```
function main(param) {
const ToneAnalyzerV3 = require('ibm-watson/tone-analyzer/v3');
const toneAnalyzer = new ToneAnalyzerV3({
  version: '2017-09-21',
  url: 'https://gateway-lon.watsonplatform.net/tone-analyzer/
  api',
  iam_apikey: 'yM29hpdmL6_VDZsxcynOnDy9pl8NW2DVUssu--Oi4_Ru',
  disable_ssl_verification: true,
});
const toneParams = {
  tone_input: { 'text': param.text },
  content_type: 'application/json',
};
return toneAnalyzer.tone(toneParams)
  .then(toneAnalysis => {
    return {toneAnalysis
    }
  });
}
```

You can now start editing the Tone_Analyzer function by replacing it with the preceding sample code in the Functions ä Actions ä Code console, as shown in Figure 7-48.

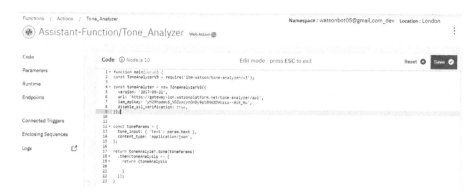

Figure 7-48. *IBM Cloud Functions showing code snippet*

Go to **Endpoints**. Under the **REST API**, copy and save the URL, as shown in Figure 7-49.

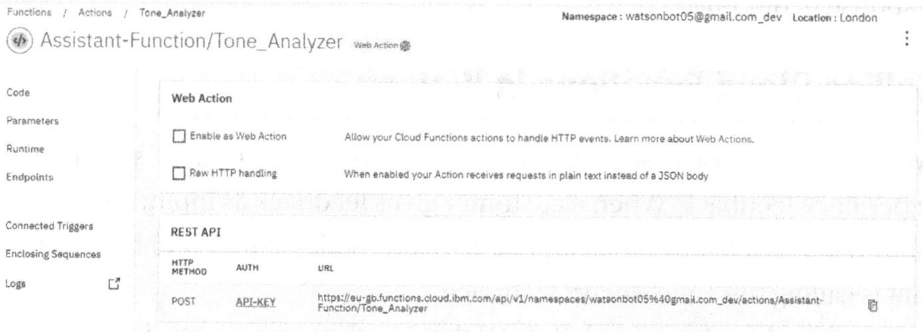

Figure 7-49. *Endpoints page*

Click **API-KEY**. Copy and save the API key, as shown in Figure 7-50.

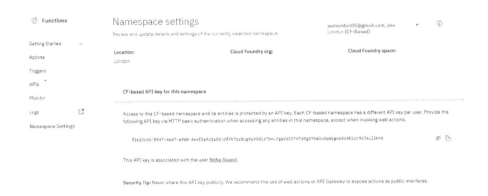

Figure 7-50. *Namespace settings page*

Now let's call this function in the skill created in the Watson Assistant service to fetch the result from the Tone Analyzer service and show the response in our bot.

Calling Cloud Functions in Watson

We have taken a use case in which we are analyzing customers' shopping experience feedback. When a customer gives feedback as input, we capture the text in a variable and pass this variable in the cloud function that is calling the Tone Analyzer service.

You can download the skill JSON that has the use case configured for Tone Analyzer.

Go to GitHub (`https://github.com/watson05/Cognitive-Bot`) to download the Tone Analyzer skill JSON.

Import the downloaded skill in the Watson Assistant Service, as explained in the Stock Market Data use case.

Once you have imported the skill, you are directed to the dialog page, where the Tone_Analyzer use case is configured (see Figure 7-51).

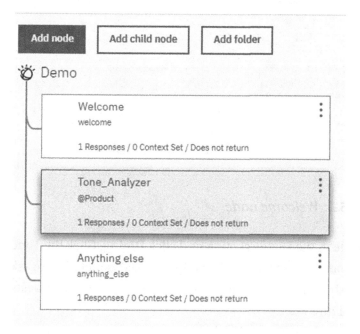

Figure 7-51. *Dialog page*

Let's look at the following components defined for the Tone Analyzer use case.

- **Entity:** @Product

- **Entity Values:** Product name, such as Bag, Laptop, Mobile Phone, Head Phone, and so forth.

We have defined the entity as @Product since we want to know what the customer bought.

We changed the default Welcome message, as shown in Figure 7-52.

Figure 7-52. *Welcome node*

Navigate to the Dialog section and click **Dialog**. Click the Tone_
Analyzer node. You see the entity defined as @Product. We are asking
for overall shopping experience feedback with a prompting question, as
shown in Figure 7-53.

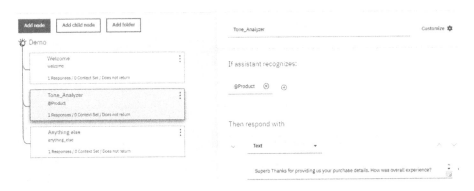

Figure 7-53. *Dialog node with filled in information*

We have captured the customer shopping experience feedback that
was given as input text in a $text context variable, which is passed in the
API, as shown in Figure 7-54.

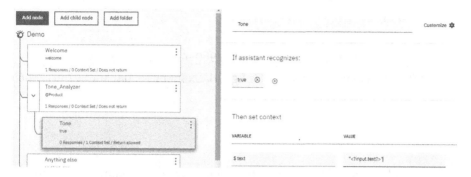

Figure 7-54. *Dialog node with information*

The following is the sample JSON that we are using to call the cloud function.

```
{
  output: {
    text: {
      values: [],
      selection_policy: sequential
    }
  },
  actions: [
    {
      name: /watsonbot05%40gmail.com_dev/Assistant-Function/
      Tone_Analyzer,
      type: cloud_function,
      parameters: {
        text: <? $text ?>
      },
      credentials: $credentials,
      result_variable: $response
    }
  ],
```

```
context: {
  credentials: {
    api_key: f2a23cdb-5947-4a67-a960-4eef2a9d2a5d:dfXh7zr
    BUgXqkG51zTGmL3gaXUi57KToRgG7HAOx8qWbgmbOU4E1UcMo7Aul2Hh6
  }
}
}
```

We'll call the cloud function in the JSON editor by clicking the Open JSON editor in the **Then set context** hamburger menu.

Replace the code in the open JSON editor, as shown in Figure 7-55.

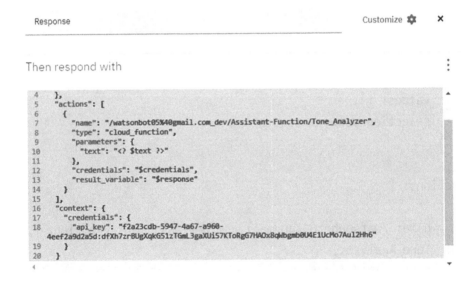

Figure 7-55. *Open JSON editor*

For the action name in JSON, you need a part of your cloud function URL, which should look similar to this:

```
https://eu-gb.functions.cloud.ibm.com/api/v1/namespaces/
watsonbot05%40gmail.com_dev/actions/Assistant-Function/Tone_
Analyzer
```

The actions section needs to be filled in the JSON editor node, like this:

```
name: /watsonbot05%40gmail.com_dev/Assistant-Function/Tone_
Analyzer .
```

To enter the credentials in the context, replace the api_key value with your Cloud Functions API key; for example, api_key: 1234567890-example

We have called the Tone Analyzer API with a shopping experience feedback parameter. Now we need to show the result fetched from the API. For this, we added a child node with the jump to **Response** from the parent node, as shown in Figure 7-56 and Figure 7-57.

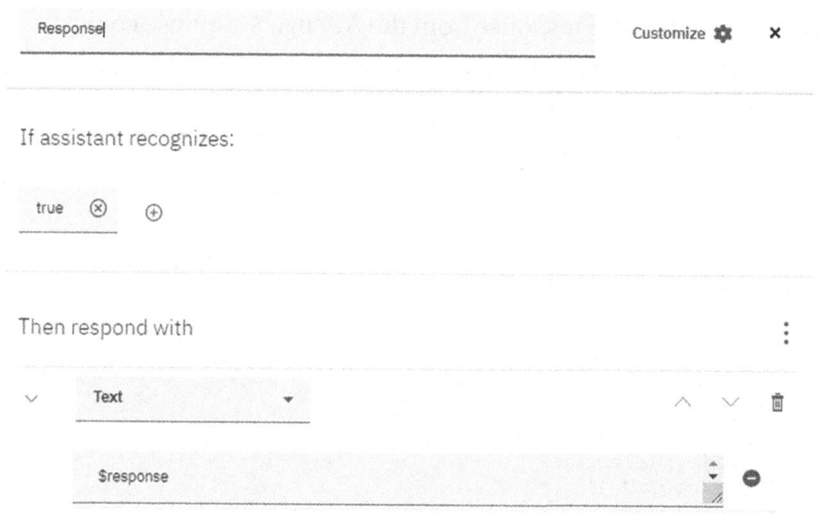

Figure 7-56. *Child node to capture the response from API*

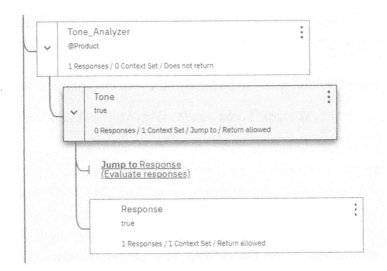

Figure 7-57. *Jump to Response*

We have fetched the response from the API in a $response context variable, which is mentioned in the result_variable, as shown in Figure 7-58.

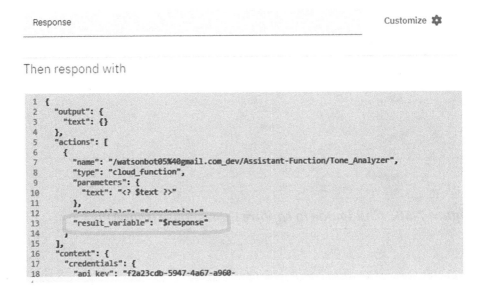

Figure 7-58. *JSON showing result_variable*

Now let's try our use case on the bot (i.e., assistant). Link the skill with the assistant, as you did earlier in the chapter. Try the use case to see tone anlayzer of customer feedback given based on their recent shopping experience, as shown in Figure 7-59, Figure 7-60, and Figure 7-61.

Figure 7-59. Testing the use case on the bot

Figure 7-60. *Result shown*

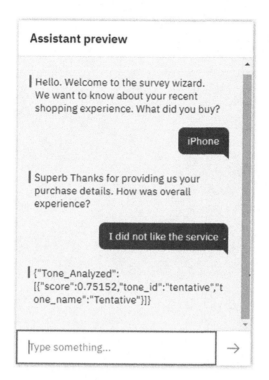

Figure 7-61. *Result shown*

Conclusion

This concludes the chapter on the various types of use cases that we can develop using built-in advanced IBM AI services to further enrich the quality of bot conversations. We created ready-to-use sample use cases for the Tone Analyzer and Watson Discovery services, and the integration of Facebook Messenger with IBM Watson.

CHAPTER 8

The Future of Cognitive Virtual Assistants

There are enterprises that have already implemented cognitive virtual assistants (CVA) and are now seeing the benefits in terms of cost savings, elevation of the user experience, standardization, simplification, and digitalization.

These organizations have been able to differentiate themselves from their competition and have raised the standards in terms of customer service, net promoter score, customer satisfaction scores, and so forth. They have been able to provide a better experience to their users by providing an intuitive way to access information and data, thus empowering them to better serve their end customers. By leveraging CVAs for partners and the ecosystem of suppliers and other stakeholders, the interface between enterprises has become simpler and faster. It has enabled quicker dissemination of information and eliminated the time waste that arises from multiple communication channels and hops.

Realizing the benefits of cognitive virtual assistants is dependent on the approach that an organization wants to take. There are organizations that have created a central ecosystem of NLP engines and a single bot

© Navin Sabharwal, Sudipta Barua, Neha Anand, Pallavi Aggarwal 2020
N. Sabharwal et al., *Developing Cognitive Bots Using the IBM Watson Engine*,
https://doi.org/10.1007/978-1-4842-5555-1_8

instance that is leveraged by all departments and functions, which is driven strategically rather than tactically. This approach provides the maximum benefit to the organization due to standardization, faster learning and adoption, experience sharing between departments, and reuse of use cases and data. This also provides a single interface to the customers, partners, and employees, albeit with applicable use cases and functionality.

Cognitive Virtual Assistants in the Future

The rapid adoption of CVAs is an indicator of how things will pan out in the future. On the one hand, enterprises are finding newer and more complex use cases for deploying CVAs; and on the other hand, technology advancement in the area of natural language, speech recognition, image recognition, text extraction, and language translation is improving with every passing day.

When it comes to the Internet-scale consumer side of the CVA story, we are already seeing rapid improvements in features, where CVAs are able to mimic language, tone, and voice, and talk to humans for specific use cases with such finesse that it becomes difficult to gauge that it is a CVA talking on the other end, and not a human being.

Currently, the state-of-the-art CVAs include personal assistants from Google, Amazon, Apple, and Microsoft. The current challenge with these personal assistants is that they are question-and-answer (Q&A) systems with limited ability to provide a context-based complete conversation experience; although Google came out with Duplex and demonstrated the capabilities of a fully human-like conversation for a few use cases.

First and foremost, future CVAs will have the ability to converse and understand not just one intent but the context of an entire conversation, including deviations from the main intent. We humans are not straightforward or predictable when we are having conversations, and thus it is challenging for a machine to decipher what is coming their way next.

A lot of AI research is spearheaded by startups, and some of them were acquired to rapidly scale up the technology through funding from technology majors. DeepMind, the creators of AlphaGo, was acquired by Google in January 2014 for $500 million. DeepMind's technology has since found its way into Google Assistant. Siri was acquired by Apple in 2010, and it now powers the virtual assistant in iPhones. Facebook bought Wit.ai in 2015; its technology is used by Facebook Messenger. Microsoft acquired Maluuba for its AI technology in the area of conversations.

The newer technologies trying to mimic the way the human brain works will make it possible for cognitive virtual agents to be more human-like in their conversations.

We also need CVAs to understand the tone and emotion behind conversations. Language is complex; the same sentence spoken in a different context or with a different tone of voice can have an entirely different meaning. The huge amounts of data that personal cognitive virtual assistants are receiving every day from humans interacting with them on a massive global scale, makes it possible to move forward and create CVAs that not only understand intent and context but also the emotions behind conversations.

Apart from personal virtual agents, the CVAs in devices and automobiles are gaining momentum. Cars and automobiles are an interesting use case because a cognitive in-car companion will look after the driver and the passengers in an unobtrusive fashion. It can hook onto the data sent from all the vehicle sensors, and it can act as a voice assistant to alert the driver and provide directions. This model is different from the auto drive model in which the automobile simply takes you from one place to another. The CVA can work in an automated mode and help passengers with things like choice of music, climate control, the best route, and other aspects of the journey.

Features like dial-home-in-case-of-emergency or dial an ambulance will be common features in a CVA, which will provide complete information in case of an accident or an emergency. Personal information about the driver and the passengers in an emergency, such as blood type and medical history, can be readily accessed by the personal assistant and help save lives.

CVAs in enterprises will soon become the single application that an employee needs to be interviewed, hired, and on-boarded, or to get work completed, submitted, and evaluated as well. The whole lifecycle of an employee—from hiring to retiring—will be handled by powerful digital assistants that are integrated with back-end ERP and HR systems. Employee service bots like DRYiCE Lucy are enabling enterprises with these features and expanding their use cases and coverage.

With these capabilities and the rapid expansion of the use cases that CVAs can accomplish, low-level tasks like booking tickets, resolving problems, serving food, managing orders, responding to email queries, solving IT problems, and so forth, will be taken over by CVAs. Conversations will be more human-like, and it will be difficult if not impossible to distinguish between a human agent and a CVA.

The CVAs will be able to emulate human behavior, such as empathy and understanding, but we must be conscious that this will be an emulation and not a human equivalent because humans are driven by emotions, whereas a CVA is using logic to understand and respond to an emotion.

In the service industry, humans are trained to recognize emotions and respond in a particular fashion if a customer is frustrated or angry, which is not a true emotion but a scripted response to make the customer feel happy. Though based on the experience of the conversation, the chances of bias of a human service assistant is much higher than a CVA.

It is also true that such innovations will trigger concerns over the impact of CVAs on human jobs and their future. However, you can think of a contrarian view in which humans have converted other humans into machines. With the advancement in technology, we are trying to reclaim human life and make it better and richer, and move humans out of tasks that are mundane and repetitive and do not leverage much intelligence.

These jobs were not automated sooner because the technology and hardware innovations required to solve these problems were complex and not scalable, even though the tasks are simpler when compared to an assembly line that manufactures automobiles.

The next frontier beyond voice recognition and understanding the emotions behind human conversations is gestures. It will not only require technology advancement to recognize gestures but essentially this will be another model of communication added back to human modes of communication. Humans will have to learn gestures, just like they learned writing and typing to communicate rather than speaking. It will be an evolution from both sides: humans using gestures and the CVAs learning to understand what they mean.

It is entirely possible that this may be completely skipped, and we move to a model where technology advances to understand and interpret our thoughts—and we don't need gestures to communicate. If this happens, the next level of advancement will be CVAs reading our thoughts and taking actions accordingly. The impact of this technology advancement will take the world by storm. It will be one more science fiction fantasy that turns to reality; but it is an amazing one.

CVAs will not be limited to question-and-answer systems or systems that aid a human in delivering what he or she desires; the next evolution in the CVA technology will be a merger of the ability of CVAs to understand instructions with the best option for the user. This will be the first step where a human not just orders but listens to what a CVA suggests. Examples of these systems are already there. Technologies like Google Maps, which guides a human rather than takes orders, or recommendation systems that suggest what users should buy, or price comparison engines that help users compare and buy products online are all available today.

The role of CVAs in applications and situations that demand collaboration and collation of data from various sources will accelerate and expand. Let's understand this with a simple example. Blocking calendars for a large number of people, organizing a meeting, and booking meeting rooms are time-consuming tasks that require access to calendar information, meeting room booking systems, and other applications. Such tasks can be easily automated by a CVA because it has access to all systems and can process the data in seconds. For a human being to do this requires multiple clicks and interfacing with multiple applications. CVAs are far more efficient than humans in repetitive monotonous tasks that require access to information and a rule base. The future is not far away when all enterprises will have a cognitive virtual agent for booking meetings. It will also keep a track of the availability of people, meeting rooms to confirm the meeting, send reminders, or suggest alternate meeting slots that are suitable for all the attendees.

These days, you may find doomsday predictions in news articles about the inevitable invention of "general-purpose AI" and the singularity, when humanity creates an AI capable of reconfiguring itself over and over again and achieving superintelligence. What happens when that becomes a reality is something that will only present itself if it happens.

But if we look at the current applications of AI, the world has moved toward "specific AI," which means a machine does one specific task and accomplishes it well, sometimes surpassing human capabilities. If we look at the AI systems created by OpenAI and DeepMind, they are capable of beating the best humans on the planet in games for which the system has been trained on. With deep learning it is becoming simpler albeit computationally and data intensive to train systems. If we extrapolate and look at the technology innovations in cognitive virtual assistants, we see the same trends—the advent of specific assistants that do limited tasks really well.

The future of cognitive virtual assistants should be much more interconnected. Different specialized bots in enterprise and personal computing spaces will work in tandem and provide simple intuitive interfaces for employees, customers, and partners. In fact, the possibility is that everyone will have their own digital personal assistants connected to specialized consumer and enterprise bots for leveraging the specific capabilities of those bots. This is akin to an API marketplace where programmers can choose specific APIs and create mashup applications.

The personal bot will have adaptors or connectors to connect to various bots, along with a mechanism to decide which specific intent or topic should go to which bot for resolution. There is no standardization today for bot-to-bot communications, but in the future, it is entirely possible that a universal bot framework and a mechanism to exchange data between bots is created and standardized. This will help address the problems of multiple bots and increase the pace of innovation in this space, with many individuals and startups creating bots for specific tasks.

The existence of a global bot, a universal interconnected hive brain that is able to see all conversations, transactions, and interactions will have both positive and negative consequences; positive in the sense that it is able to connect both environments. The first is the physical environment of the planet we live in, and the second one includes the objects that we have created in the digital environment in the form of processes and systems, data, and so forth. Such an ecosystem will have the potential to simplify and change the lives of everyone on the planet by automatically completing transactions, setting reminders, coordinating between people and processes, processes and other processes, people and other people, and machines and other machines. Personal bots will talk through this universal API to other bots and complete things that humans do by talking to others, emailing, and meeting people.

Bots will handle many of our mundane daily tasks in the home and in the workplace. They will progress to independently evaluate situations and solve problems by providing proactive suggestions rather than being reactive. The ability of bots to integrate with massive back-end databases and machine learning engines will lead to a situation where the bot knows more about the environment by virtue of faster processing of data and access to a larger and better database. The role of the CVA will evolve from something that sits passively and gives suggestions to something that makes decisions on behalf of a human. That will be a tipping point when humanity and machines switch roles.

On the flip side, the universal bot will know everything about everyone. Imagine the power of the universal bot to change preferences of people, to alter the way we think, to try and alter our social and political views slowly but surely by feeding us the information that best suits its needs rather than ours. Imagine the power of the data that resides with the universal bot; it knows the emotions and intent of people at a global scale and cannot use it to advance a particular agenda, or manipulate the economic and political systems but perhaps alter humanity forever.

Index

© Navin Sabharwal, Sudipta Barua, Neha Anand, Pallavi Aggarwal 2020
N. Sabharwal et al., *Developing Cognitive Bots Using the IBM Watson Engine*,
https://doi.org/10.1007/978-1-4842-5555-1

Printed in the United States
By Bookmasters